MY FIRST BRITANNICA

Plants

10

ENCYCLOPÆDIA
Britannica®

CHICAGO   LONDON   NEW DELHI   PARIS   SEOUL   SYDNEY   TAIPEI   TOKYO

International Standard Book Number: 1-59339-048-3 (set)
International Standard Book Number: 1-59339-058-0 (volume 10)

My First Britannica:
Volume 10: Plants 2004

Britannica.com may be accessed on the Internet at http://www.britannica.com.

Plants

TABLE OF CONTENTS

Sunflower
© Ron Watts/Corbis

Plants

INTRODUCTION

Can trees ever bounce? Is the tomato a fruit or vegetable? What crop was buried with the Egyptian pharaohs? Could you walk on a water lily without sinking?

In Volume 10, *Plants,* you'll discover answers to these questions and many more. Through pictures, articles, and fun facts, you'll learn about the great diversity of plant life found around the world.

To help you on your journey, we've provided the following signposts in *Plants*:

■ **Subject Tabs** — The coloured box in the upper corner of each right-hand page will quickly tell you the article subject.

■ **Search Lights** — Try these mini-quizzes before and after you read the article and see how much - *and how quickly* - you can learn. You can even make this a game with a reading partner. (Answers are upside down at the bottom of one of the pages.)

■ **Did You Know?** — Check out these fun facts about the article subject. With these surprising 'factoids', you can entertain your friends, impress your teachers, and amaze your parents.

■ **Picture Captions** — Read the captions that go with the photos. They provide useful information about the article subject.

■ **Vocabulary** — New or difficult words are in **bold type**. You'll find them explained in the Glossary at the back of this volume. And there's a complete listing of all Glossary terms in the set in the **Reference Guide and Index**, Volume 13.

■ **Learn More!** — Follow these pointers to related articles throughout the set.

And don't forget: If you're not sure where to start, where you saw something before, or where to go next, the **Reference Guide and Index** (Volume 13) will point the way.

Have a great trip!

MY FIRST BRITANNICA

DID YOU KNOW?
Many types of bird love sunflower seeds. Birdwatchers often use the seeds to attract yellowhammers, bullfinches, and other birds to gardens.

The Golden Giants

The sunflower gets its name from the way it turns its head, or bloom, from east to west to follow the Sun. The name is fitting for another reason too - the bloom itself looks something like the Sun.

The sunflower is a plant from the Americas. About 400 years ago, the French explorer Samuel de Champlain saw American Indians growing sunflowers on the eastern shore of Lake Huron, one of the Great Lakes. The Indians had a variety of uses for the sunflower plant.

The sunflower is as useful today as it was back then. Sunflower leaves can be used as **fodder** to feed animals. The flowers produce a yellow dye. As food, sunflower seeds are a good source of protein and vitamin E. They can be eaten dried or roasted. Milled seeds can be used to make bread or a coffee-like drink. Pressed seeds yield oil that is comparable to olive or vegetable oil. The oil is used for cooking and for making soaps and paints.

The sunflower is a giant among flowers. Its rough and hairy stem grows from 1 to 4 metres tall. Its broad leaves range from 8 to 30 centimetres long.

The bloom of a sunflower has two parts. The central **disk** flowers are dark. The ray flowers surrounding the central disk are golden yellow. As the plant ripens, the seeds develop in the disks. Sunflowers grown on farms can have disks that are 30 centimetres wide.

SEARCH LIGHT

As food, sunflower seeds are a good source of which vitamin?

LEARN MORE! READ THESE ARTICLES…
AMERICAN INDIANS (VOLUME 4) • TULIPS (VOLUME 10)
VINCENT VAN GOGH (VOLUME 3)

Although it is related to the little daisy, the sunflower is one of the largest and most splendid of flowers. The sunflower plant is valuable for its economic uses as well as for its beauty.
© Ron Watts/Corbis

Answer: They're a good source of vitamin E.

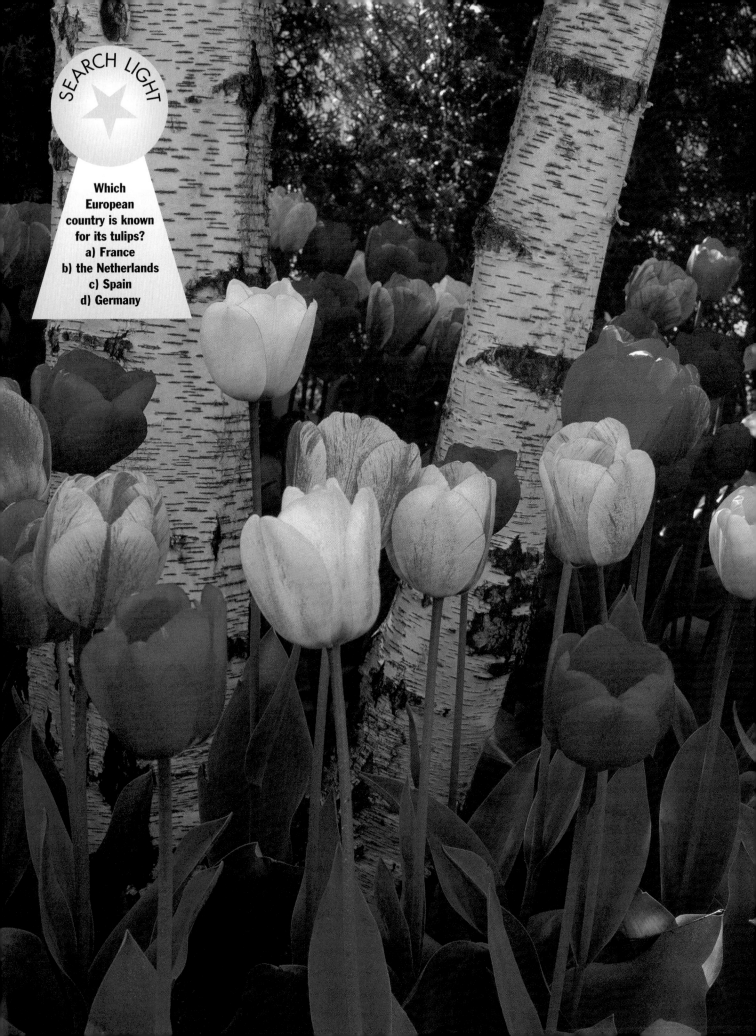

SEARCH LIGHT

Which European country is known for its tulips?
a) France
b) the Netherlands
c) Spain
d) Germany

From Bulbs to Beauties

Did you know that there are nearly 4,000 kinds of tulip? These flowers come in almost every colour. There are white tulips and yellow tulips, red tulips and pink tulips, orange tulips and purple tulips. You can even find black tulips and brown tulips!

Tulips are cousins of the lilies. They grow from bulbs that are planted in the ground. The bulbs are thick buds. They are like tightly packed bags that hold all the things a plant needs to keep it alive during the cold winter months.

Two girls amongst tulips in a field.
© Mike Zens/Corbis

The inside of a bulb has layer upon layer of thick moist padding surrounding a small tough stem. When the sun is just warm enough and the ground is just wet enough, this stem starts to press its way up through the top of the bulb and out of the ground. While the flowering tulip waves in the breeze, the bulb below is soaking up more food and water, and new bulbs are forming. These can be collected to plant later.

The people of Turkey were probably the first to grow tulips in their gardens. The name 'tulip' came from the Turkish word *tulbend*, which means '**turban**'. The flower's shape was said to look like this cloth headdress.

An **ambassador** from Austria took tulips from Turkey to Europe for the first time, in 1551. The tulips grew very well in his city, Vienna. But the flowers grew even better in Holland. Soon the Dutch people were famous for their tulips. Today millions of people all over the world buy tulip bulbs from the Netherlands, as Holland is called today.

LEARN MORE! READ THESE ARTICLES...
AUSTRIA (VOLUME 6) • THE NETHERLANDS (VOLUME 6)
SUNFLOWERS (VOLUME 10)

DID YOU KNOW?
When tulips were introduced to Europe, they instantly became popular there. Because they were rare at that time, the bulbs were very expensive. People bought, sold, and traded them the same way we do today with valuable things such as gold.

Growing tulips is popular among home gardeners and is a major industry in the Netherlands. The flower is valued for its early spring bloom, its brilliant colours, and its graceful shape. Here, beautiful red and yellow tulips surround the trunks of birch trees.
© Darrell Gulin/Corbis

Answer: b) the Netherlands

Garden Royalty

The rose is probably the most popular flower in the world. For its sweet scent and its delicate petals of various colours, the rose is known as 'the queen of flowers'.

Wild roses are found in the Northern **Hemisphere,** mainly in regions that are not too hot or too cold. Most of the roses people grow in gardens

A flowering hybrid tea rose.
© Patrick Johns/Corbis

originally came from Asia. Other wild varieties are found in North America, while a few grow in Europe and north-western Africa.

The plant grows as an upright shrub or as a vine that grows along the ground or climbs. Shrub roses can be grown either as large bushes or as miniature plants with tiny blossoms. Climbing roses can be **trained** to grow on walls and fences.

The stems of most rose plants have thorns as well as flowers. The flowers range in colour from white through various shades of yellow and pink to dark crimson and burgundy.

Some gardeners try hard to come up with new colours or colour combinations. They take roses from different places and breed them together. This produces new types called hybrids. While wild roses generally have five petals per flower, many hybrids are double roses with many petals. One of the most popular hybrids is the tea rose. The tea rose exists in a range of colours and has large well-shaped tea-scented blossoms.

Most roses are enjoyed simply for their beauty, but some are used to make products. A sweet-smelling oil called 'attar' is made from rose blossoms and is used in perfumes. Rose flowers also have a part near their base called a rose hip, which is a source of vitamin C.

DID YOU KNOW?
Breeders have tried for many years to come up with a blue rose, but they have not succeeded.

LEARN MORE! READ THESE ARTICLES…
ASIA (VOLUME 7) • TEA (VOLUME 10) • TULIPS (VOLUME 10)

Climbing roses grow up the side of a castle wall in Kent, England.
© Patrick Ward/Corbis

Answer: The tea rose smells like tea.

The Sweet Bloomer

Honeysuckle is a plant that's popular with both birds and people. Birds love the colourful juicy berries, which grow red, orange, or black. People love the sweet-smelling flowers.

There are more than 200 kinds of honeysuckle. Some of them are tall bushes. Some are climbing vines, and others trail along the ground. Most honeysuckles grow berries. Some have **evergreen** leaves, while others have leaves that change colour with the seasons.

The pretty trumpet honeysuckle is a popular climber in North America. It has orange-red flowers with yellow centres. The berries

Yellow-orange honeysuckle.
© Michael Boys/Corbis

are bright red. The Tatarian honeysuckle is a common kind that grows as a bush. It has rose-pink or white flowers that bloom in late spring. Its bright red berries appear during the fall. This honeysuckle grows mostly in Europe and Siberia (a region in Russia).

The sweet honeysuckle can be seen in Europe, Asia, and the United States. This plant bears red-orange berries. Its flowers are purple-white. They're the favourite flowers of hawk moths. The Japanese honeysuckle comes from eastern Asia, but it has been taken to many other areas. It has sweet-smelling whitish flowers and black berries. It is very sturdy and **flourishes** in all kinds of weather, dry or damp, hot or cold.

Honeysuckles are a real benefit to **wildlife managers** because deer, rabbits, wild turkeys, quail, and songbirds love to eat their leaves, stems, and berries. And many people plant honeysuckle in their gardens to attract colourful butterflies and hummingbirds.

LEARN MORE! READ THESE ARTICLES...
BIRDS (VOLUME 11) • RABBITS AND HARES (VOLUME 12) • ROSES (VOLUME 10)

An orange honeysuckle grows in western Washington state. The honeysuckle's sweetly fragrant flowers have made it a long-standing favourite in the garden.
© Mike Zens/Corbis

DID YOU KNOW?

In some places it's illegal to sell or distribute Japanese honeysuckle. This kind of honeysuckle grows so well it can grow right over other plants and shut out the light they need. It's often considered a weed.

Answer: TRUE.

Floating Stars

An American Indian folktale says that the water lily was once a star. It fell from the sky, and when it struck the water, it changed into the beautiful flower we see floating in shallow ponds and slow-moving streams.

The water lily is a very interesting plant. Its leaves float on top of the water, and its thick stems reach beneath the water's surface to the mud at the bottom. Each plant has a single flower attached to a **stalk**. The flowers bloom above the water. They float so gracefully that it's easy to see how they could be described as floating stars.

The lily plant also produces a fruit. It looks like a nut or a berry. Inside are seeds that will sink or float away to produce new plants.

Some water lilies open only in the morning. Others open only in the evening. The mysterious Egyptian lotus, for example, has white flowers that bloom in the night and stay open only until midday.

One common water lily is the **fragrant** water lily. It has sweetly scented white flowers tinged with pink. These lilies are **native** to eastern North America, but today they are **cultivated** all over the world.

People often grow water lilies to decorate garden ponds. One person who did this was the French painter Claude Monet. His beautiful paintings of water lilies are widely admired. But lilies also provide food for fish and other water animals. And the floating leaves are a favourite resting place for frogs!

LEARN MORE! READ THESE ARTICLES...
AMERICAN INDIANS (VOLUME 4)
FROGS (VOLUME 11) • RUSHES AND REEDS (VOLUME 10)

DID YOU KNOW?
The largest water lily in the world is a kind that grows in the Amazon River valley. The leaves of this plant can measure up to 1.8 metres across—and they're strong enough to support the weight of a small child!

Blooming white and pink lotuses float on the surface of a pond.
© Bohemian Nomad Picturemakers/Corbis

Answer: Claude Monet is known for painting water lilies.

SEARCH LIGHT

How are orchids different from other flowers?

Exotic Flowers

Orchid plants are known for their **exotic** and beautiful flowers. The flowers often smell very sweet. They grow in a wide range of colours, including red, purple, yellow, white, and green. Some orchids also have bright markings or patterns on them.

There are tens of thousands of different kinds of orchid. They grow best in warm, wet, tropical areas. But orchids can be found all over the

Flowering orchids.
© Hal Horwitz/Corbis

world, except near the North and South poles. Many of them are grown in South America, Southeast Asia, the Philippines, and Australia and then sold to other countries.

Some orchids live in soil, but most tropical orchids grow on other plants such as vines or creepers. The roots of these orchids have a spongy cover. This lets the orchids soak up all the water they need from the air around them. Different orchids develop in different ways. Most get a new stem each year that sprouts sideways from the main stem. Others have a single stem that gets taller every year. Some orchids have single flowers, while others have clusters of flowers. Some orchid flowers are tiny. Others are very large.

All orchid flowers have one petal that is separate from the rest. It is called the 'lip', and it's different in shape and colour from the other petals. The lip is what makes orchids different from all other flowers.

Their rare beauty makes orchids very popular with flower collectors. Orchid lovers sometimes pay a lot of money for a single orchid stem. Collectors have even been known to steal orchids from one another!

LEARN MORE! READ THESE ARTICLES…
PHILIPPINES (VOLUME 7) • RAINFORESTS (VOLUME 1) • TULIPS (VOLUME 10)

Orchids are found nearly worldwide and are particularly abundant in the tropics. They are amongst the favourites of flower lovers around the world.
© Hal Horwitz/Corbis

Answer: One petal is separate from the rest. It is called the 'lip'.

SEARCH LIGHT

How
does the
pitcher plant
kill insects?

Bugs Beware!

The plant called the Venus fly trap may look harmless enough. But it isn't, at least not for flies! If a fly or other insect touches part of the plant's leaves, it will be captured. On the end of each leaf is a trap. These traps are hinged like jaws and can open and close. Sharp spines that look like teeth line the edges. And very sensitive hairs are inside. If a fly brushes against one of these tiny hairs, the trap will snap shut, with the fly caught inside.

The Venus fly trap is not the only kind of plant that catches insects. It is one of several types of carnivorous - or 'meat eating' - plants. Most plants get all the things they need to grow from the soil, air, water, and sunshine. But carnivorous plants have adapted to living in soil that doesn't give them everything they need. They get the rest from the insects they catch.

Of course, these plants don't chew and eat food the same way you do. Parts of the plants ooze liquid chemicals that dissolve, or break apart, the insects. The plants then absorb, or soak up, the substances they need.

Carnivorous plants have all sorts of clever traps and tricks for catching insects. The pitcher plant has leaves shaped like small pitchers, or jugs. The insides of these leaves are very slippery. And the plant produces a sweet juice called 'nectar' to attract insects. When an insect climbs in to taste the nectar, it slips and slides to the bottom of the leaf. It drowns in the liquid at the bottom and is slowly digested.

LEARN MORE! READ THESE ARTICLES…
ANTS (VOLUME 11) • CACTUS (VOLUME 10)
INSECTS (VOLUME 11)

DID YOU KNOW?

Some people think that there are plants big enough to eat people. But there aren't any plants that big. No plants eat people - except in films.

Fruit of Gold

A banana plant may grow to a height of 6 metres or more, but it is considered to be an **herb** rather than a tree. Instead of a trunk, it has a **stalk** made up of leaves rolled tightly around each other. From the stalk grows a big bunch of 50 to 200 individual bananas. Only one bunch grows on each plant. The bunch is made up of several clusters. Each cluster has 10 to 20 bananas. After harvesting, the plant is cut down. A new one then grows from an underground stem.

Farm worker on a banana plantation in Oman, in the Middle East.
© Christine Osborne/Corbis

Bananas grow only where it is warm and wet all the time, which is why people in cold countries may never see a banana plant. They love to eat the bananas, though. That's why banana farms called **plantations** are a big business in South Asia, Africa, Central and South America, and the islands of the Caribbean Sea. But Asia is where bananas originally came from.

Most everyone knows what happens to a banana that has sat around too long. It gets brown and mushy. So bananas have to be picked while they're still hard and bright green. They may have a long trip ahead of them - usually thousands of kilometres from the plantation to the grocery store. Refrigerated ships keep the bananas from ripening too soon, and then special heat and moisture treatments help them to ripen on schedule.

Bananas are used in making delicious cream pies, cakes, breads, and fruit salads. Many people's favourite banana dessert is the banana split ice-cream treat. But not all bananas are eaten as fruit. Some varieties never get sweet. These bananas, called 'plantains', are cooked and served as a vegetable.

LEARN MORE! READ THESE ARTICLES...
CENTRAL AMERICA (VOLUME 9) • MANGOES (VOLUME 10) • MONKEYS (VOLUME 12)

DID YOU KNOW?

The largest banana split ever made was reported to be a little over seven kilometres long.

Bunches of bananas hang on a plant before being harvested and exported from the Caribbean island of Grenada in the West Indies.
© Dave G. Houser/Corbis

Answer: a) bananas that aren't sweet.

Vegetables or Fruit?

Cooks call the tomato a vegetable, but gardeners say it's a fruit. It's actually both! In the garden the tomato is considered a fruit because it grows from a flower and has seeds in it. But in the kitchen it's considered a vegetable because it isn't sweet like apples or grapes.

Tomatoes were first grown thousands of years ago by South American Indians who lived in the Andes Mountains. In Mexico, Indians **cultivated** tomatoes long before Spanish explorers arrived in the 1500s. The name 'tomato' comes from *tomatl*, a word in the language of the Aztec people of Mexico.

The Spanish who returned to Europe after their explorations brought the tomato back with them. The tomato was first used as a food in Spain and Italy. From Europe, tomatoes were taken to North America. Today they grow all around the world, wherever winters are not too cold and summers not too hot.

Tomatoes not only taste good - they're also good for you! They're packed with vitamins A and C. Tomatoes can be served cooked by themselves or used as a part of many different meals. They're used to make soups and salads. Tomato juice is popular because of its tangy flavour. Tomatoes also form the base for ketchup, chilli sauce, and spaghetti sauce. And, of course, they're a must for your pizza!

A few tomato varieties.
© Michelle Garrett/Corbis

LEARN MORE! READ THESE ARTICLES…
ANDES (VOLUME 9) • LUTHER BURBANK (VOLUME 4) • GRAPES (VOLUME 10)

A father and his son taste a tomato they have just picked. Tomatoes come in many different shapes and sizes.
© Ariel Skelley/Corbis

DID YOU KNOW?

For a long time the tomato was believed to be a relative of the poisonous belladonna plant. In fact, the roots and leaves of the tomato plant are poisonous. But the fruit is safe to eat and, in fact, is very good for you!

Answer: c) Spanish and Italians.

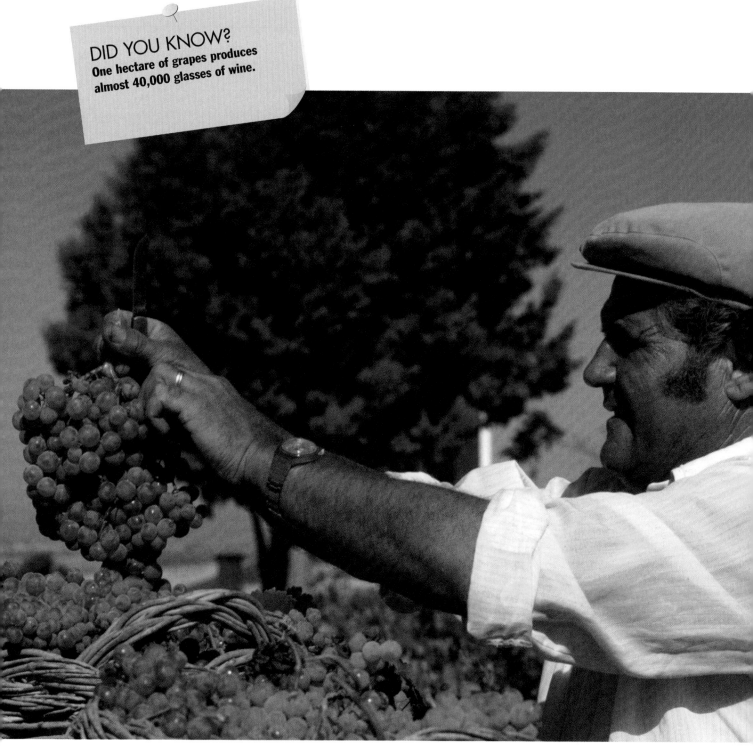

This worker is collecting bunches of grapes
at harvest time. Green and red table grapes are
an excellent source of vitamin A.
© Ted Streshinsky/Corbis

Fruit of the Vine

Grapes grow wild in wooded and warmer regions of the Northern **Hemisphere**. And people have raised grapes in these regions for thousands of years. Grapes have been taken to South Africa, South America, and Australia and grown with great success. There are about 60 different grape plants, as well as thousands of varieties.

The grape plant is a woody vine. A vine is a kind of plant that can't stand up by itself. It has stems called tendrils that cling to things and support the plant. An untrimmed vine may reach a length of 15 metres. Grapes are berries that grow in bunches on the vine. Grapes come in many colours - pale green, yellow, red, purple, or black. Some grapes have a white powdery coating.

SEARCH LIGHT

The growing
of grapes
is called
a) 'vineculture'.
b) 'viticulture'.
c) 'grapiculture'.

The growing of grapes is called 'viticulture'. People don't usually grow grapes by planting seeds. Instead, they take cuttings off a vine that is already growing. These cuttings spend a year or so in **nurseries**, waiting to grow roots. When they have roots, they're ready to grow outside.

Table grapes.
© Craig Lovell/Corbis

Another method of grape growing is called layering. In layering, the branch of a full-grown vine is bent into a curve and made to grow along the ground. New shoots and roots soon grow from this part of the branch. These are cut off from the parent vine and replanted as new vines.

Grapes are high in sugar. Different types are used for different purposes. Some are eaten fresh. Others are dried out to make raisins. But most are squeezed for their juice. Some grape juice is put through a process called 'fermentation' that changes some sugar into alcohol. The product that results is called 'wine'.

LEARN MORE! READ THESE ARTICLES...
AESOP'S FABLES: ANIMAL STORIES THAT TEACH (VOLUME 5)
FRANCE (VOLUME 6) • STRAWBERRIES (VOLUME 10)

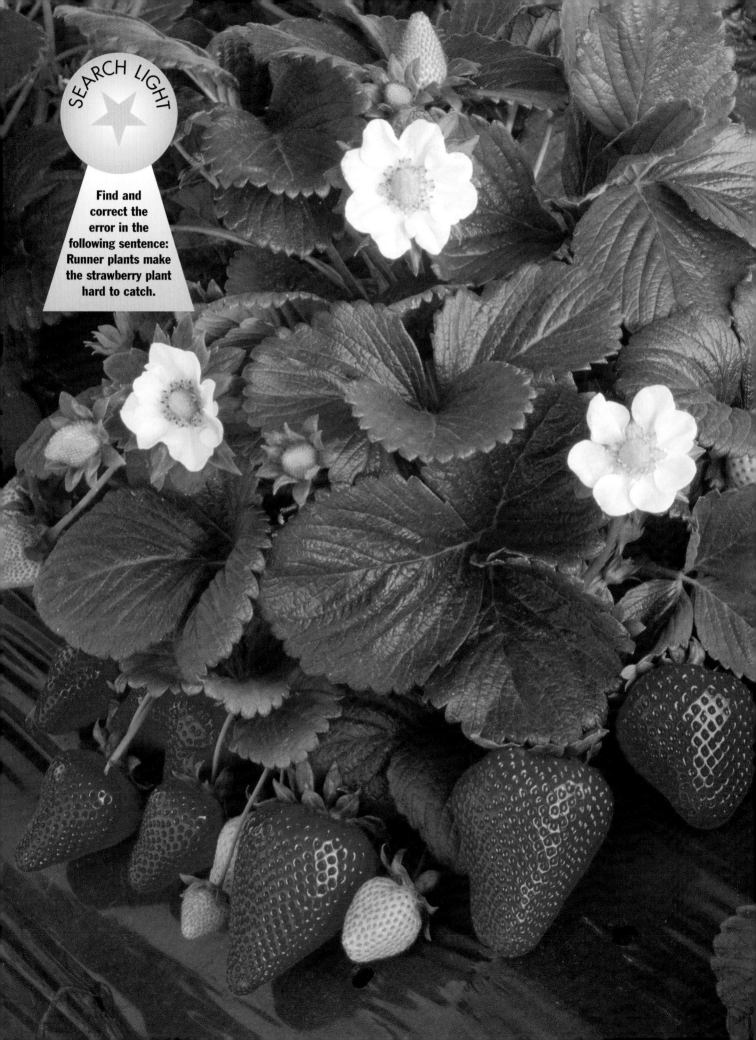

SEARCH LIGHT

Find and correct the error in the following sentence: Runner plants make the strawberry plant hard to catch.

Luscious Fruit Treat

Strawberries are eaten fresh, often with cream. They are also used as a filling for pastries, tarts, and cakes. Strawberry shortcake is made of fresh strawberries, a cake or biscuit base, and whipped cream. Needless to say, strawberries are a very popular fruit.

Strawberry plants can be found throughout most of the United States and Canada, Europe, the United Kingdom, and parts of Africa. They are also grown in New Zealand, Australia, and Japan.

The strawberry is a low **herb** plant that branches off in all directions. At the top of the plant is the 'crown' from which the leaves sprout. The leaves have three sections, each of them hairy with **saw-toothed** edges. The flowers are mostly white and sometimes reddish. They appear in small groups on slender **stalks** arising from the leaves. As the plant gets older, the roots become woody. Then the crown sends out 'runner plants', trailing vines that spread over the ground, making the plant bigger.

Runner plants are planted in autumn for a crop expected the following year. Strawberry plants are usually used to produce fruit for one to four years. In regions with very cold winters, the plants are put out in spring and protected during winter by covering the rows with straw.

Strawberries need to be stored in a cool and dry place after they've been picked. But they still don't remain fresh for very long. Some are frozen or preserved to make them last longer.

LEARN MORE! READ THESE ARTICLES…
LUTHER BURBANK (VOLUME 4) • GRAPES (VOLUME 10)
HONEYSUCKLE (VOLUME 10)

The heart-shaped red fruits of the strawberry plant are popular all over the world.
© Ed Young/Corbis

Answer: Runner plants make the strawberry plant bigger.

The 'Head' of a
Vegetable Family

Cabbage has been grown for food since ancient times. Nearly 3,000 years ago, the Greek poet Homer mentioned it in his story-poem the *Iliad*.

Wild cabbage is native to the shores of the Mediterranean Sea. It also grows wild on the sea cliffs of Great Britain. The ancient Romans probably

Two heads of cauliflower.
© Ed Young/Corbis

planted it there. Cabbages have thick moist leaves with a waxy coating. The leaves are often grey-green or blue-green in colour. Cabbage plants like cool weather and deep rich soil.

Over hundreds of years, many vegetables have been developed from the wild cabbage. Some are used for garden decoration or for feeding animals. But people eat many kinds. The cabbage group includes the common cabbage, cauliflower, broccoli, Brussels sprouts, and several other vegetables. They are rich in vitamins and minerals and low in **calories**.

The common, or head, cabbage has a tight bunch of leaves (the head) around a centre stem. People eat the leaves raw or cook them. Cabbage soup is a popular dish in much of eastern Europe. Finely chopped raw cabbage is the main ingredient in a salad called 'coleslaw'. If sliced-up cabbage is salted and put away for a long time, it goes through a chemical change. The result is sauerkraut, a popular dish in Germany. In Korea cabbage is a major ingredient in the traditional dish called *kimchi*.

Cauliflower has a head of tight thick white flowers. People eat the flowers either raw or cooked. Broccoli has bright green loosely clustered flowers. People eat these flowers along with the tender stalks. Brussels sprout plants have many little cabbage-like heads instead of one large head at the top.

LEARN MORE! READ THESE ARTICLES
BRUSSELS, BELGIUM (VOLUME 6) • KOREA (VOLUME 7)
MEDITERRANEAN SEA (VOLUME 1)

DID YOU KNOW?
In France a popular term for a loved one is *petit choux*, which means 'little cabbage'.

There are more than a hundred varieties of cabbage.
Common (or head) cabbage is pictured here.
© Eric Crichton/Corbis

When Is a Nut Not a Nut?

SEARCH LIGHT

Find and correct the errors in the following sentence: Peanuts are legumes that grow on trees in cold sandy places.

They look and taste like nuts. They have shells like nuts, and they have skins like nuts. But they're not nuts. They're *peanuts*.

Actual nuts grow mostly on trees or bushes. But peanuts grow underground. That's why peanuts are also called 'groundnuts'. Although they look and taste like nuts, peanuts are really part of a plant group called 'legumes'. Legumes also include peas and beans. The peanut pod is a spongy shell covered with tiny dimples. Inside the shell you will usually find two peanuts. These are the seeds for new peanut plants.

A woman harvests peanuts on the island of Mauritius.
© Wolfgang Kaehler/Corbis

Peanuts grow easily in warm sandy places. They require at least five months of warm weather, with rainfall during the growing season. The peanut plant is a low bush. Some kinds grow long low branches called 'runners'. When the peanuts are ripe, peanut farmers usually dig up the plants and stack them against sticks to dry out. Farmers feed the tops of the dry plants to their animals.

Peanuts may be roasted in their shells before they're eaten. Or they may be shelled and prepared as salted peanuts. Roasted peanuts are used in sweets and baked goods, for peanut butter, and in many other foods. Peanuts are often grown just for their oil.

An important person in the history of the peanut is Dr. George Washington Carver. This American researcher suggested that farmers plant peanuts to help make their worn-out soil healthy again. And then he came up with new uses for peanuts so that the farmers could sell them. By the time he'd finished, Dr. Carver had found more than 300 things that could be made out of peanuts.

LEARN MORE! READ THESE ARTICLES...
NUTS (VOLUME 10) • SENEGAL (VOLUME 8)
UNITED STATES: A WEALTH OF RESOURCES AND BEAUTY (VOLUME 9)

Peanuts are grown in warm temperate or subtropical areas throughout the world. Here workers pick weeds in a peanut field in Samoa.
© Catherine Karnow/Corbis

DID YOU KNOW?
Dr. George Washington Carver's products from peanuts included peanut milk, cheese, and coffee, as well as plastics, shampoo, and shoe polish.

Answer: Peanuts are legumes that grow underground in warm sandy places.

Tasty Tubers

Fill in
the gap:
The part of a
yam that is eaten
grows _____.

Yam plants are climbing vines. Long slender stems bear clusters of small green flowers that look quite pretty. The plants need hot wet weather and take rather long to grow. Different varieties of them are grown as food in the tropics.

In some parts of West Africa and New Guinea, yams are also used in ceremonies related to farming.

Baskets of yams at a market in the Cook Islands.
© Robert Holmes/Corbis

Yams, like potatoes, have thick tubers. A tuber is the thick part of the plant's stem that grows underground and stores food for the plant. And just as with the potato, the tuber is the part of a yam that people eat.

There are hundreds of varieties of yam. They differ greatly in look and taste. The colour of the tuber's flesh may be white, yellow, pink, or purple. Some taste sweet, some bitter, and some quite bland.

True yams are different from the sweet potato. However, some varieties of sweet potato are often called yams in the United States. Both sweet potatoes and yams are **starchy** foods with a fair amount of sugar in them. Some yams also contain poisons that may make a person sick if the tuber is not properly cooked. The poisons are destroyed by cooking.

Most people eat yams as they would potatoes. Yams are served fried, roasted, baked, and boiled. Cooked yams are often mashed into a sticky paste or dough that can then be further baked or boiled.

LEARN MORE! READ THESE ARTICLES...
AFRICA (VOLUME 8) • PEANUTS (VOLUME 10) • PEPPERS (VOLUME 10)

Women collect yams in Papua New Guinea.
© Caroline Penn/Corbis

Hot and Spicy

Garden peppers have been used in cooking since ancient times. Hot peppers contain a substance called 'capsaicin' that gives them a sharp burning taste. Many people enjoy this strong taste and use it to flavour foods. People like to eat peppers fresh, dried, smoked, tinned, powdered, and pickled.

Pepper plants are herbs. The fruit of the plants differs in size, shape, and taste. The colour ranges from green through yellow to deep red and purple. You'll find peppers in the tropics of Asia. They also grow all over Central and South America. In 1493 pepper seeds were carried from South America to Spain. After that, the plants quickly spread all over Europe.

There are two general types of peppers: the mild and the hot varieties.
© Paul Almasy/Corbis

There are two kinds of pepper: mild and hot. Mild peppers are usually large and can be red, green, or yellow in colour. Bell peppers are bell-shaped, wrinkled, and puffy. Pimiento is a mild pepper with a special flavour and is usually used for stuffing other foods, such as olives. Paprika is another mild pepper. It's usually powdered and used as a spice. It is especially popular in Spain and Hungary.

The hot peppers include cherry, red cluster, tabasco, long chilli, and cayenne peppers. These are often served as relishes and pickles or ground into a fine powdered spice. Tabasco peppers are ground and mixed with vinegar to make a spicy hot sauce. Both fresh and dried Mexican chilli peppers are used to flavour stewed meat dishes.

LEARN MORE! READ THESE ARTICLES...
MEXICO (VOLUME 9) • THAILAND (VOLUME 7) • TOMATOES (VOLUME 10)

SEARCH LIGHT

Fill in the gap: _____ is what makes hot peppers hot.

Bell peppers like the ones shown are often used in salads, as cases for fillings, and in other cooked dishes.
© Michelle Garrett/Corbis

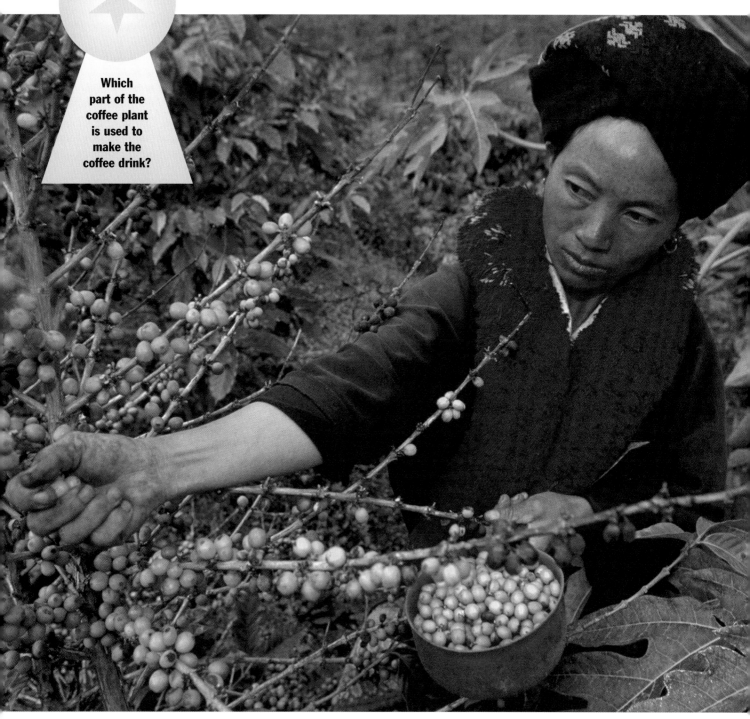

More than 10 billion coffee trees are grown on plantations all over the world. Each tree yields about 450 grams of coffee every year. Trees begin to bear fruit when 3 to 5 years old and continue to do so for another 10 to 15 years. Here, a woman in Thailand handpicks coffee cherries, which contain coffee beans.

© Michael S. Yamashita/Corbis

36

The World's Favourite Cup

Coffee is one of the most popular drinks in the world. Many people think it has a great taste and a wonderful smell. Coffee also contains caffeine, which is a stimulant - that is, a substance that increases the body's activity.

Coffee grows as a bush with sweet-smelling flowers and fleshy fruit called 'coffee cherries'. Within the fruit are two seeds, or 'beans'. The

Coffee beans ready for purchase.
© Mark Ferri/Corbis

beans are dried, roasted, and ground. The ground coffee is then **brewed** in water to make a drink. Coffee plants need warm weather and plenty of rain, so they grow only in **tropical** regions. There are at least 60 types of coffee plants. But only two kinds, called Arabica and Robusta, are in great demand.

Arabica coffee has more flavour and **fragrance**. It is grown in Central and South America, the Caribbean, and Indonesia. Coffee from Colombia is especially well known. Robusta coffee is grown mainly in Africa. The Robusta plant does not pick up disease easily. It is also useful in making instant coffee. Instant coffee is coffee powder that dissolves completely in water.

Coffee probably first came from Ethiopia, in north-eastern Africa. From there it was taken to the Middle East. At first it was used as a food, as a medicine, and in wines. People did not begin to drink coffee as we know it for hundreds of years. Coffee was taken to Europe and then the Americas starting in about the 1500s.

Today coffee is one of the world's most popular drinks. Rest periods taken during working hours are often called 'coffee breaks'. Many, many people begin each day by drinking a cup of coffee.

DID YOU KNOW?
Many countries have special coffee drinks. Turkish coffee is a strong, thick sweetened drink. Italy's espresso is made by forcing steam through ground coffee beans. France's café au lait and Latin America's café con leche both mean 'coffee with milk'.

LEARN MORE! READ THESE ARTICLES...
COLOMBIA (VOLUME 9) • INDONESIA (VOLUME 7)
VIENNA, AUSTRIA (VOLUME 6)

Answer: The coffee seeds, or beans, are used to make coffee.

SEARCH LIGHT

What's the difference between green tea and black tea?

The Cup That Cheers

It soothes you when you are upset. And if you're tired, it can lift your spirits. It's tea - the drink that cheers!

Tea was first drunk in China thousands of years ago. At first it was used as a **medicinal** drink, but eventually it became popular to drink anytime. It was later introduced to Japan. European trading ships took it from Asia to England and Holland.

Worker separating tea leaves by hand in Indonesia.
© Owen Franken/Corbis

There are two main varieties of tea - the small-leaved China plant and the large-leaved Assam plant. Mixing the leaves of these produces many other types of tea.

Tea can be named according to where it's grown. For example, there's China tea, Ceylon tea, Japanese tea, Indonesian tea, and African tea. But most tea is known as green, black, or oolong tea. Green tea, made from the China plant, is produced in Japan, China, Malaysia, and Indonesia. Black tea, made from the Assam plant, comes mostly from India. Oolong teas are produced mostly in southern China and Taiwan.

The different kinds of tea are made in different ways. To make black tea, the freshly picked leaves are dried, rolled, and strained. They are then fermented. Fermenting is a way of making the flavour more intense. Finally, the leaves are dried with hot air. This is how the tea becomes black. Unlike black tea, green tea is not fermented. The leaves are just rolled and dried, so they remain green. Oolong is made like black tea. It is sometimes scented with flowers such as jasmine.

Tea is made ready for drinking by soaking its leaves in boiled water. This is called 'steeping'.

LEARN MORE! READ THESE ARTICLES...
CHINA (VOLUME 7) • COFFEE (VOLUME 10)
LEAVES (VOLUME 1)

DID YOU KNOW?
Iced tea was made popular by an Englishman at the St. Louis World's Fair of 1904 in the United States. His job was to get people to drink tea. The weather was hot, so he filled tall glasses with ice and poured hot tea over it. Everyone loved it!

Tea is made from the young leaves and leaf buds of tea plants. The farmworkers shown here are harvesting tea leaves in Malaysia.
© Neil Rabinowitz/Corbis

Answer: Aside from their different colours, black tea is fermented and green tea is not.

DID YOU KNOW?
The French term for 'potato' is *pomme de terre*, which means 'apple of the earth'. This may be because apples and potatoes have a similar texture (feel), size, and shape.

Fruit Tree Royalty

The apple tree is a hardy plant that is grown in more parts of the world than any other fruit tree. That's why the apple has often been called the 'king of fruits'.

Even though it is five-sixths water, the apple has vitamins, minerals, and **carbohydrates**. Before the science of nutrition told us how to eat healthily, people already knew that 'an apple a day keeps the doctor away'.

Colourful apple varieties.
© Royalty-Free/Corbis

Apples are grown for eating, cooking, and making juice. 'Eating' apples are crisp and juicy, with a tangy smell. They may be red, green, greenish yellow, pink, or orange. 'Cooking' apples are firm. 'Juice' apples are used to make apple juice and cider. Apples are also preserved as jams, jellies, apple butter, and chutneys. And applesauce - made by stewing and, often, sweetening apples - is popular in many places.

If you plant the seeds of a good-tasting apple, you will probably be disappointed by the fruit that the new tree produces. Branches, as well as seeds, have to be used to produce the best apples. The process is called 'grafting'. Apple trees need well-drained soil to grow. They also need a period of cool winter weather to rest before the fruit-growing season.

There are many signs that humans discovered the apple a long time ago. There are pictures of apples carved on stone by **Stone Age** people. Apples are mentioned in the Bible. Although some kinds of apple grow wild in North America, the apples Americans eat come from varieties that were brought from Europe. John Chapman, an early American planter better known as Johnny Appleseed, helped to spread these varieties far and wide. Apple pie, in fact, is a symbol of America.

LEARN MORE! READ THESE ARTICLES…
ATLAS: BEARER OF THE WORLD (VOLUME 5) • LUTHER BURBANK (VOLUME 4)
ORANGES (VOLUME 10)

SEARCH LIGHT

Why is the apple called the 'king of fruits'?

Apples must be handled carefully to avoid bruising. Here a worker gently picks apples ready for harvesting.
© Royalty-Free/Corbis

Answer: The apple is called the 'king of fruits' because apple trees are grown in more places than any other fruit tree.

DID YOU KNOW?
Fruit bats help spread mangoes by carrying the fruit to another perch, where they eat the flesh and drop the seed. The seed plants itself in the ground, and soon a small mango tree pops up there.

The Regal Tropical Fruit

Sweet, tasty, and wonderfully sticky - that's a mango! So many people like this fruit that it is sometimes called 'the queen (or king) of **tropical** fruits'. And not only does it taste good - it's good for you because it's full of vitamins.

But mangoes didn't always taste so good. Thousands of years ago they were small fruits that tasted like pine needles! At that time they grew only in some parts of Asia, such as India and Myanmar. Today they're grown in most tropical countries. There are even mango farms in the southern United States.

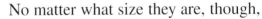

Fresh mangoes.
© W. Wayne Lockwood, M.D./Corbis

Mangoes come in many shapes, sizes, and colours. They can be oval or round or long and slender. They can be red, yellow, or green. The smallest mangoes are no bigger than plums. The biggest are up to 25 centimetres long and can weigh as much as 2.3 kilos.

No matter what size they are, though, all mangoes have a lot of very juicy yellow or orange fruit underneath a thin skin. In the middle of the fruit is a single flat seed.

Mangoes grow on tall trees. Take five elephants and put them on top of each other, and that's how high mango trees can grow. The trees are evergreen, which means they keep their leaves all year.

You can eat mangoes raw. Just wash them, peel them, cut them, and eat them. Or you can eat mangoes mixed in milk, like a mango smoothie. Mangoes are also used to make sauces and chutneys. In India, during festivals, you'll find mango leaves strung together hanging outside the front doors of many houses. This is because mangoes are believed to bring luck.

LEARN MORE! READ THESE ARTICLES...
BANANAS (VOLUME 10) • INDIA (VOLUME 7) • JACKFRUIT (VOLUME 10)

The mango is one of the most important and widely grown fruits of the tropical world. Mangoes are a rich source of vitamins A, C, and D.
© Douglas Peebles/Corbis

Answer: TRUE. Long ago they had a chemical flavour. Unripe mangoes still have that taste.

43

SEARCH LIGHT

Fill in the gap: The _____ is one of the most valuable palms in the world.

The leaves of palms are usually clustered at the top of the tree's trunk in a large fan- or feather-shaped crown. The palm trees shown here are growing on a beach in St. Croix.

The Prince of Plants

The palm is one of the most useful plants around, which is why people sometimes call it the 'prince of the plant kingdom'. There are many types of palm. They grow as trees, shrubs, and vines in the tropics and other warm regions.

The trunk of the palm is branchless, with a **tuft** of large leaves on the top. The trunks can be very tall, or they can be so short that the plant is almost trunkless. Often the palm trunk is smooth. But the trunks of some are spiny like a cactus while others are covered with stiff **fibres** that can be made into strong cords. Palm leaves are **pleated** and may be shaped like fans or feathers. Some varieties of palm leaves are very long with prickly tips.

Palm trees grow from sand on a beach in Jamaica.
© Eye Ubiquitous/Corbis

Palms produce dry or fleshy fruits that vary in size, shape, and structure. For example, the date and the betel nut are soft fleshy fruits. The fruit of the coconut is hard on the outside and has moist 'meat' and liquid inside. The coco-de-mer is the largest fruit in the world. This palm fruit can be larger than a human head, with a pair of seeds that look like two coconuts joined together.

The coconut is one of the most valuable palms in the world. It provides vegetable oil for cooking. The fibre of the coconut husk is called 'coir' and can be woven into ropes and mats. The coconut shell is hard and is used to make cups and bottles. The liquid in the centre is called 'coconut milk'. You can drink it and cook with it, much as you would with animal milk.

LEARN MORE! READ THESE ARTICLES…
NUTS (VOLUME 10) • OASIS (VOLUME 1)
SRI LANKA (VOLUME 7)

DID YOU KNOW?
Some island people say there are as many uses for coconuts as there are days in a year.

Answer: The coconut is one of the most valuable palms in the world.

SEARCH LIGHT

What colour are lemons when they are picked from the tree?

Sweet, but Oh So Sour!

The lemon is a **citrus** fruit, a family of fruits that includes limes, grapefruit, and oranges. Lemons grow on small trees and spreading bushes. The trees can grow quite tall if they are not trimmed. Their leaves are reddish when young, but they gradually turn green. Some lemon trees have sharp thorns next to the leaves.

Lemon flowers are large and may grow singly or in small clusters. The new buds of the lemon flower have a reddish tint. As they blossom, the inside of the flower turns white. Lemon flowers have a lovely sweet scent. This is one of the reasons that people like to have lemon trees in their gardens.

Lemon trees bloom throughout the year. The fruit is usually picked while it is still green. It can be damaged easily, so pickers wear gloves and have to be careful when handling the fruit. The fruit is stored for three or more months until its colour has changed to an even yellow.

The lemon fruit is oval and covered with a **rind** that is yellow when ripe. Inside, the flesh (or pulp) is divided into eight to ten segments that contain small pointed seeds. The pulp and its juice are rich in vitamin C. Lemon flavour is used in many foods, and many people put it in their tea. But the juice is very sour.

Some other important products provided by the lemon are lemon oil and pectin. In some places, the oil is used in perfumes and soaps. Pectin is what makes jelly so thick and sticky. It is also used in some medicines.

LEARN MORE! READ THESE ARTICLES…
MEDICINE (VOLUME 2) • ORANGES (VOLUME 10) • TEA (VOLUME 10)

DID YOU KNOW?
The substance that makes lemons so sour is called citric acid. In addition to being so sour, it is a very harsh substance - in fact, it's said that there's enough citric acid in a lemon to dissolve a pearl!

Beautiful and fragrant, lemon trees usually bloom throughout the year.
© Ray Juno/Corbis

Answer: Lemons are usually picked while they are still green. They turn yellow after they have aged for a while.

47

SEARCH LIGHT

Can you name three citrus fruits?

The Drinkable Fruit

The orange is one of several kinds of small trees and shrubs that belong to the **'citrus'** group. Other common citrus fruits are lemons, limes, grapefruit, and tangerines. The first oranges and other citrus fruits probably grew in the tropical regions of Asia, especially in the islands of Southeast Asia. The practice of growing oranges spread to India, to the east coast of Africa, and then to the Mediterranean regions. Today oranges are also grown in the warm regions of the Americas and Australia.

The orange is a nearly round fruit with a leathery, oily peel and juicy flesh (or pulp) inside. It grows on attractive trees 4.5 to 9 metres tall. Orange trees have sweet-smelling waxy blossoms and leaves that stay green throughout the year. Their branches often have small thorns as well. A single orange tree will bear fruit for 50 to 80 years or longer. Sometimes the age of an orange tree is counted in centuries!

The most popular variety of orange is the China orange. It's also called the sweet orange or common orange. This orange tastes best when it is fully ripe, and it should not be picked before that. Another popular variety, the Seville orange, is not as commonly grown. The Seville is used in making **marmalade**. Other varieties of oranges include the Jaffa from Israel, the blood orange with its red pulp, and the navel, which is usually seedless.

Oranges are also grown to produce juice, either fresh or frozen. Nearly half the oranges produced in the United States are made into frozen **concentrated** juice. Orange juice is rich in vitamin C and also provides some vitamin A.

LEARN MORE! READ THESE ARTICLES…
ISRAEL (VOLUME 7) • LEMONS (VOLUME 10)
UNITED STATES: A WEALTH OF RESOURCES AND BEAUTY (VOLUME 9)

> **DID YOU KNOW?**
> There's no English word that rhymes with 'orange'. Try it for yourself!

The seedless navel orange, shown here, became a major fruit in California after it was introduced from Brazil in 1873.
© Ed Young/Corbis

Answer: Oranges, tangerines, lemons, limes, kumquats, and grapefruit are all citrus fruits.

Fig trees grow only in hot dry climates. Shown here is
the fruit of the fig tree as it ripens.
© Richard T. Nowitz/Corbis

Poor Man's Food

In Mediterranean countries the fig is used so widely, both fresh and dried, that it is called the 'poor man's food'. The soft juicy fruit of the fig tree cannot remain fresh for long in the hot **climate** where it grows. So it has to be dried in the sun before it is sent to the market. Fresh or dried, the fig is packed with food value.

Figs were first found growing around the Mediterranean Sea. It's no surprise then that figs still grow in the countries bordering the Mediterranean—including Turkey, Greece, Italy, and Spain. Spanish missionaries introduced the fig tree to Mexico and California. The entire fig crop in the United States comes from California.

There are four main types of figs: caprifig, Smyrna, White San Pedro, and Common. When a fig is introduced into another country, a new name is often given to it. The Smyrna fig became known as the Calimyrna fig in California.

Fig plants are either bushes or small trees. Fig trees are easily grown from **cuttings** off an adult tree. The fruit occurs either singly or in pairs. The trees produce two or three crops a year.

The best-tasting dried figs are those that have been allowed to dry partly on the tree. The figs are then laid out on trays to finish drying in the sun. Turning and moving them about while they dry improves their quality. Most dried figs are eaten in their natural form, though many are ground into a paste to be used in bakery products.

SEARCH LIGHT

Why would the fact that so many people eat figs earn it the nickname 'poor man's food'? (Hint: Food costs money.)

LEARN MORE! READ THESE ARTICLES...
LIBYA (VOLUME 6)
MEDITERRANEAN SEA (VOLUME 1)
OLIVES (VOLUME 10)

DID YOU KNOW?
There are more than 900 members of the fig group. One of them, the Bo tree, or pipal, is sacred in India. It is believed to be the tree under which the Buddha sat when he attained enlightenment.

Answer: Poor people can't afford many kinds of food but can always eat the figs found growing wild.

51

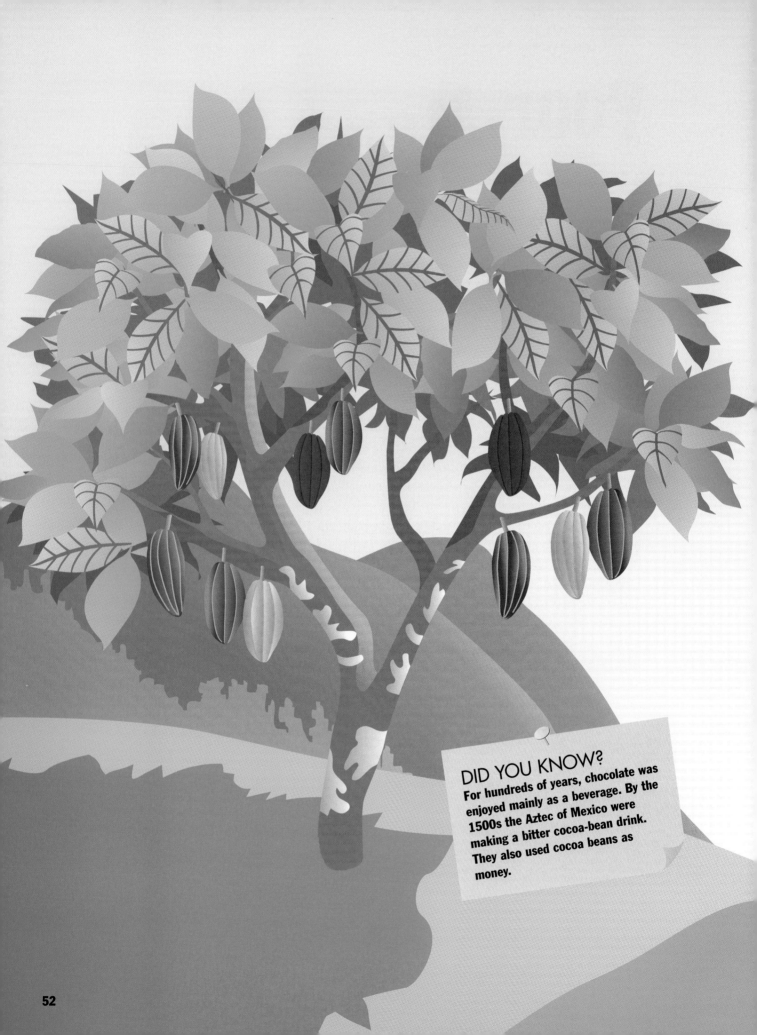

DID YOU KNOW?
For hundreds of years, chocolate was enjoyed mainly as a beverage. By the 1500s the Aztec of Mexico were making a bitter cocoa-bean drink. They also used cocoa beans as money.

The Chocolate Tree

A chocolate tree may sound like something made up in a book or film, but chocolate really does come from trees. A tree called the 'cacao' is the source of all cocoa powder and chocolate.

Cacao trees grow only in warm areas that get a lot of rain. The trees grow long fruit called 'pods' that range in colour from bright yellow to deep purple. Inside the pods are rows of seeds called 'cocoa beans'. Each is about the size and shape of a big fingernail. It is from these cocoa beans that we get one of the world's favourite foods, chocolate.

But a lot of things have to be done to the beans before they turn into chocolate. After the cocoa beans are taken out of the pods, they are left in a damp place for a few days. The beans turn a rich brown colour and begin to smell like chocolate. Then they are dried and cleaned.

Next the beans are shipped to chocolate factories all over the world. There they are roasted and ground into a paste. This paste contains a fatty yellow liquid called 'cocoa butter'. To make chocolate, you have to add extra cocoa butter to the paste. To make dry cocoa powder, you have to remove all the cocoa butter.

The chocolate is still not ready to eat, though. Cocoa beans are not naturally sweet. In fact, the paste is very bitter. So a lot of sugar must be mixed in. Milk may be added too. The chocolate is then poured into moulds to harden into chocolate bars. Now it is finally ready to eat!

LEARN MORE! READ THESE ARTICLES…
COFFEE (VOLUME 10) • MEXICO (VOLUME 9)
SWITZERLAND (VOLUME 6)

SEARCH LIGHT

True or false? Chocolate is naturally very sweet.

Answer: FALSE. Chocolate is naturally quite bitter. It is the sugar added to it that makes it sweet.

SEARCH LIGHT

Most fruit grows on branches. Where does jackfruit grow?

The Largest Tree-Borne Fruit

The largest fruit that grows on trees is the jackfruit. And when we say it grows on trees, we mean it - the fruit grows on the main trunk of the tree and not on the branches. That's because it is so heavy that the branches can't support it - they would break right off!

So how big is this fruit? Well, a single jackfruit can weigh over 36 kilos! It sometimes reaches 90 centimetres long and almost 60 centimetres around. The jackfruit tree is also very large. It looks something like a large oak tree and grows to a height of 15 to 20 metres.

A young Indonesian boy carrying jackfruits.
© Bennett Dean—Eye Ubiquitous/Corbis

Jackfruit grows in the warm regions of Asia. It's grown widely in tropical countries where it is warm and rains a lot, such as the Philippines. There are many varieties of jackfruit. Some of the popular ones include Black Gold, Galaxy, and Honey Gold.

Like its cousin the mulberry, jackfruit is a compound fruit. This means that it has many, many seeds and that each seed surrounded by its **pulp** is a separate fruit. The big jackfruit you see is like a huge container holding all the little fruits together.

Young jackfruits are green. They turn brownish yellow when ripe. Raw jackfruit is cooked like a vegetable, though the sweet pulp surrounding the seeds can be eaten fresh. The seeds can be boiled or roasted and eaten like chestnuts.

Jackfruit has other uses too. The wood is a valuable hardwood like teak. It is used for making many things, especially furniture. Dried jackfruit leaves are used as fuel for cooking fires, while the green leaves provide **fodder** for goats.

DID YOU KNOW?

Ripe jackfruits have a strong odour before they're cut open. Some people compare the smell to that of rotting onions! But once you cut into the ripe fruit, it smells more like pineapples or bananas.

LEARN MORE! READ THESE ARTICLES...
ASIA (VOLUME 7) • BANANAS (VOLUME 10) • PHILIPPINES (VOLUME 7)

**Jackfruit is a distant cousin of the fig.
It can grow to tremendous size.**
© Liu Liqun/Corbis

Answer: Jackfruit grows on tree trunks. It's too heavy for branches.

55

Spectacular Leaves, Sensational Syrup

In parts of the United States and Canada autumn is spectacular as the leaves on the trees turn bright yellow, red, and orange. One tree in particular displays fantastic autumn colours - the maple. Some maple trees even display unusual colours such as burgundy, bronze, and purple.

There are about 200 kinds of maple tree. They can be found throughout most of North America, Europe, and north-eastern Asia. The leaves of most maples grow thickly in a **dome** shape. In summer the thick **foliage** of the maple provides lots of shade. This makes it a popular tree for parks and streets. Many people also plant maple trees in their gardens.

The fruit of maple trees is a hard pebble-sized structure with a pair of thin wings. Each wing has a seed at its tip. The wings help the seeds 'fly' away on the wind, far enough from the tree to grow in the sunlight.

Many maples produce sweet **sap**. In North America the sap of the sugar maple is made into maple syrup. Sugar maples grow slowly. They do not produce sap until they are about 40 years old!

North American Indians long ago learned the secret of tapping maple trees for their sugar. The process is fairly simple. Several holes are drilled into the bark of the tree. **Spouts** are driven into these holes, and the sap flows through the spouts into pails hanging on the spouts. The sap is boiled until it has thickened. Then the maple syrup is ready to pour onto your pancakes!

LEARN MORE! READ THESE ARTICLES...
AMERICAN INDIANS (VOLUME 4)
NORTH AMERICA (VOLUME 9)
RUBBER TREE (VOLUME 10)

DID YOU KNOW?
Even though maple sap flows through the trees all spring, summer, and autumn, it is collected for syrup only in the early spring. That's when the trees produce the sweetest sap.

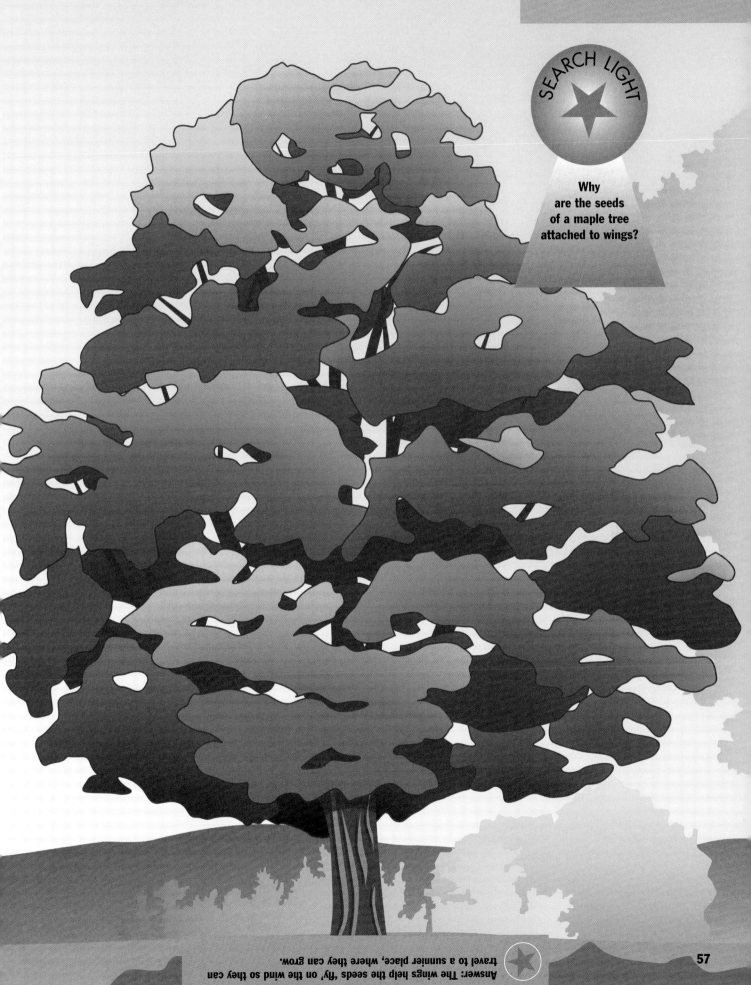

Why
are the seeds
of a maple tree
attached to wings?

Answer: The wings help the seeds 'fly' on the wind so they can
travel to a sunnier place, where they can grow.

The Original Fast Food

Before people learned to hunt or fish, they lived mostly on fruits, nuts, and berries. Nuts were especially important because they are very nourishing and rich in oil and protein. Nuts also keep well and are easy to store. A nut is actually a kind of fruit. It is dry and hard, and it is usually covered with a tough woody shell.

DID YOU KNOW?
The kola nut, grown widely in the tropics, has been used to flavour fizzy drinks. But many of these drinks now contain chemicals that taste like the kola nut instead.

A couple of nuts that you may know about are chestnuts and pistachios. There are several kinds of chestnut tree, including the American, European, Chinese, and Japanese varieties. Chestnuts are an important food for people and animals. The American and European chestnuts provide valuable wood. And some chestnut trees are grown simply for their beauty.

Pistachio trees are from Central Asia, where they have been grown for about 3,000 years. Today they are also grown in North America. Their nuts are greenish and very tasty.

Other kinds of nuts include hazelnuts, beechnuts, and acorns. But some foods that are popularly called 'nuts' aren't true nuts. Peanuts, for example, are actually a type of bean! And coconuts are really a kind of stone fruit called a 'drupe'. The Brazil nut is also called the candlenut because it can be lit and used as a candle. But it's technically a seed.

Walnuts are another 'nut' that's not really a nut. But they too are good food. They have been grown since ancient times. They were highly valued in Persia and Mesopotamia. Today they are grown in many countries. Black walnut trees are also planted as decorations, and their fruit **husks** are used for making dyes. The trees grow slowly and may live for more than 250 years!

LEARN MORE! READ THESE ARTICLES...
IRAN (VOLUME 7) • PALM (VOLUME 10) • PEANUTS (VOLUME 10)

Some foods that are called 'nuts' are actually other kinds of foods. These include walnuts and coconuts.
EB Inc.

Groves of olive trees cover the hills near the city of Jaén in southern Spain.

SEARCH LIGHT

True or false? People eat olives right off the tree.

Plant of Peace and Plenty

Since ancient times people have grown olive trees for their fruit and oil. Today olive trees are found in all the countries bordering the Mediterranean Sea. The trees are also grown in parts of the United States, Australia, and South Africa. But the leading producers of olives and olive oil are Spain, Italy, and Greece. They sell a lot of the fruit and oil to other countries.

Olive branches ripe with fruit.
© Vittoriano Rastelli/Corbis

The common olive tree has broad leaves and many branches. Its leaves are dark green above and silvery underneath. Olive branches have been a **universal** symbol of peace since the days of ancient Greece.

Olive trees bloom in late spring. The tiny white flowers hang in clusters and develop into fruit that is either picked by hand or shaken from the tree. An olive tree does not always bear fruit every year. The trees may produce a heavy crop one year and no crop the next year.

Often the olives are picked when they are still unripe and green coloured. Some crops are allowed to ripen and darken on the trees before they're picked. But fresh olives are very bitter. Before they can be eaten, they must be treated with chemicals and stored, sometimes for several months. By the time they're ready to eat, their colour may be green, black, dark red, or even purplish.

Olives are grown for the production of olive oil as well. The oil is taken from the fruit. It is one of the most widely used oils for cooking and eating, especially by people in the Mediterranean region. In using this oil, they are carrying on a tradition that is as old as civilization.

LEARN MORE! READ THESE ARTICLES…
GREECE (VOLUME 6) • MEDITERRANEAN SEA (VOLUME 1) • PALM (VOLUME 10)

DID YOU KNOW?

The olive tree is an evergreen and keeps its leaves all year-round. It can grow to be 15 metres tall and may live more than 500 years!

Answer: FALSE. Olives are bitter right off the tree and have to be processed before they can be eaten.

Find and correct the errors in the following sentence: The tallest of the Earth's 100 kinds of grasses can grow 100 metres high.

A family enjoys a walk hand in hand through a grassy park. Many people like the look, feel, and smell of a clean fresh lawn of grass.
© Steve Thornton/Corbis

Nature's Carpets

Most flowering plants grow from the tip of the stem. Grass is different. The part that grows is at ground level. That's why grass isn't usually hurt by munching cows or lawnmowers. The grasses make up a successful plant family with almost 10,000 different kinds now living.

Tall grass in a plain in Nebraska, U.S.
© Macduff Everton/Corbis

Grasses come in all sizes. A blade of lawn grass may be only about three centimetres high. A giant timber bamboo, by contrast, can grow to a height of 30 metres. The grass family includes wheat, rice, and maize - the **cereal** grains that are the world's most important food sources.

Grasses have adapted to a wide range of **climates**, from the tropics to the high Arctic. Grasses grow on the rainforest floor and on mountain slopes. They can also be found in saltwater and freshwater marshes. However, there are certain areas called 'plains' and 'steppes' where grasses rule! A plain is like an ocean of tall grass, rippling in the wind. A steppe is a drier kind of grassland with shorter grass.

Most grass leaves have ribbon-shaped blades. Some tropical grasses, though, have broad oval blades. The leaves of desert grasses are stiff and harsh and are often rolled inward. Some are even bristly and thorny. Grasses that grow in the water have waxy leaves that **repel** water.

Many grasses provide food for animals, both tame and wild. But some grasses become weeds that are not at all welcome.

LEARN MORE! READ THESE ARTICLES…
BAMBOO (VOLUME 10) • MARSHES (VOLUME 1)
RICE (VOLUME 10)

DID YOU KNOW?
Grasses have flowers, but they are usually small and don't appear at all unless the grass is allowed to 'grow out'.

Answer: The tallest of the Earth's 10,000 kinds of grasses can grow 30 metres high.

63

DID YOU KNOW?
Bulrush leaves can be used to stop and fill cracks in barrels and boats because the leaves swell up when they get wet.

Marsh Plants

Rushes and reeds are grassy plants that grow in wet places such as marshes. For thousands of years, people all over the world have found many everyday uses for these plants.

Rushes are flowering plants with a round tube-like **stalk** and hollow leaves. They can be found in or near water in parts of the world that have cold winters. There are many kinds of rush. The common rush is often used for weaving chair seats, mats, and baskets. The inside of the stalk is used for making wicks for oil lamps and **tallow** candles. These are often called 'rushlights'.

The bulrush grows in water and reaches a height of 2.5 metres above the surface. It provides food and cover for wildlife. People use bulrush leaves for making mats, baskets, chair seats, and ropes. The yellow pollen of the flowers is sometimes used for flavouring biscuits and pancakes. And the flowering spikes can be boiled and eaten like corn on the cob.

Reeds are grasses that grow along the edges of lakes, pools, marshes, and streams, from the cold Arctic to the warm tropics. They can be 5 metres tall. They have feathery clusters of flowers and smooth stiff stems.

Since ancient times, people of various cultures have used dried reed stems for building huts and **thatching** roofs. Reeds have also been used for making baskets, arrows, pens, and musical instruments. One kind of reed, papyrus, was used by the ancient Egyptians to make one of the earliest forms of paper.

LEARN MORE! READ THESE ARTICLES…
GRASSES (VOLUME 10) • MARSHES (VOLUME 1) • PAPER (VOLUME 2)

SEARCH LIGHT

Reeds and rushes can grow almost wherever there is
a) dirt.
b) water.
c) sun.

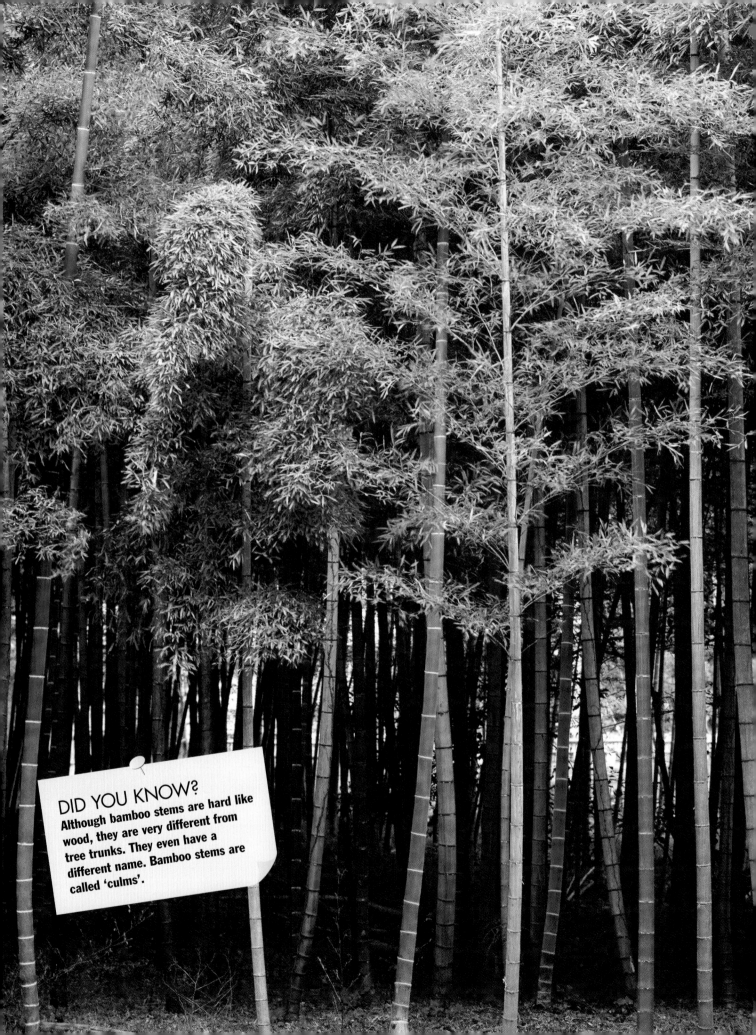

DID YOU KNOW?
Although bamboo stems are hard like wood, they are very different from tree trunks. They even have a different name. Bamboo stems are called 'culms'.

The Tallest Grass

Bamboo may grow as tall as a tree, but it is actually a kind of grass. Bamboo looks like a tree too, growing straight and thin, with branches at the top. Some kinds of bamboo grow to a height of 40 metres. Others grow so fast that they add more than 30 centimetres to their height in one day!

Not everything about bamboo happens fast, however. Some plants will not produce flowers and seeds until they have grown for as long as 120 years! After blooming only once, such a plant dies. Other kinds of bamboo bloom and produce seeds every year.

There are more than 1,000 kinds of bamboo. Most are found in East Asia and Southeast Asia. Some kinds grow in the southern United States along riverbanks and in marshes. The plants grow best where it's warm and rainy.

Bamboo is one of the world's most useful plants. Many people in warm countries build rafts, bridges, and houses from bamboo. Their floor mats and furniture are bamboo as well. The hollow stems of bamboo can be joined together and made into pipes to carry water. The stems can also be split to make all kinds of tools and utensils. Bamboo flutes make music. Bamboo sprouts and shoots are used in Asian cooking. And bamboo can be mashed into a pulp to make paper.

People aren't the only ones who put bamboo to good use. The giant panda of China will eat almost nothing else.

© Dave Bartruff/Corbis

© Nevada Wier/Corbis

(Top) Bamboo's hollow stems;
(bottom) Vietnamese boys crossing a river
on a footbridge made from bamboo.

SEARCH LIGHT

Which of
the following
are uses
for bamboo?
making paper
building houses
piping water
building furniture
feeding pandas

LEARN MORE! READ THESE ARTICLES…
BANGLADESH (VOLUME 7) • PANDAS (VOLUME 12) • RUSHES AND REEDS (VOLUME 10)

Most species of bamboo grow in Asia and on islands of
the Indian and Pacific oceans.
© Royalty-Free/Corbis

SEARCH LIGHT

Fill in the gap: Barley was one of the _____ plants grown as a crop.

A Versatile Cereal

Barley was one of the first plants ever grown as a crop. Like other food plants in the group called 'cereals', barley is a grass that is grown for its **starchy** seeds. Barley has a nutty taste and a lot of food value. People have known for a long time that barley is good to eat. It was probably first

Barley, one of the world's major cereal plants.
© Doug Wilson/Corbis

grown in **prehistoric** Ethiopia and in Southeast Asia. Egyptian farmers grew barley as far back as 5000 BC. Ancient people of Europe, Asia, and North Africa raised it too.

Barley is an especially widespread crop because it can be grown in so many different climates. It grows and ripens quickly, which makes it just right for areas that have short growing seasons - regions far to the north (such as Canada) or high up in the mountains (such as Tibet). But barley can survive just as well in the dry heat of North Africa.

Ancient people used barley to make bread. Although barley doesn't bake as well as wheat does, the flour is good for making flat breads such as pita. And barley is ideal for making some hot cereals. Polished **kernels** called 'pearl barley' serve to thicken and flavour soups. Barley can also be put through a process that turns it into a flavouring called 'malt'. Barley malt is used in making some vinegars and drinks, especially beer.

Despite all these uses, only about half the barley grown in the world is eaten by people. The rest goes to feed animals.

DID YOU KNOW?
Ancient Roman gladiators trained on a diet of barley. These professional fighters gained energy and strength from barley's excellent food value.

LEARN MORE! READ THESE ARTICLES...
CZECH REPUBLIC (VOLUME 6) • ENERGY (VOLUME 2) • ETHIOPIA (VOLUME 8)

About half of the world's barley crop is used as animal feed.
© Frank Lane Picture Agency/Corbis

Answer: Barley was one of the first plants grown as a crop.

Grain of the
Americas

Maize is a grain, just as wheat and rice are. Maize is known as 'corn' in the United States, Canada, and Australia. It was first found in the Americas. Mayan farmers of Mexico and Central America **cultivated** maize. Early European explorers of the Americas were the first to take maize to Europe. Since that time, maize has been grown all over the world.

A boy holding ears of corn in a farm field in South Africa.
© Barbara Bannister–Gallo Images/Corbis

Maize grows in areas that have rich soil and cold nights but no frost during the growing season. It also needs plenty of sunshine to ripen. These conditions are found in a large area of the midwestern United States known as the Corn Belt. Similar conditions are also found in parts of Asia, much of Central and South America, the Mediterranean, and southern Africa. The largest producers of maize, after the United States, are China and Brazil.

Maize is used to feed cattle and **poultry**. And, of course, it serves as food for humans. The maize that people eat is also called 'sweet corn'. The grains of maize that people eat are the seeds of the plant. The seeds are called 'kernels' and are found along the length of the spike. The spike with the kernels is commonly known as the 'ear' of corn. Leaves called 'husks' wrap around and cover the spike. The seeds, if they are planted, will grow into new maize plants.

Large quantities of maize are used in Latin American cooking. *Masa harina* is a kind of flour made from maize. It makes a dough that's used to make tortillas - a kind of round thin flat bread. They are the wraps for tacos, burritos, and enchiladas.

LEARN MORE! READ THESE ARTICLES...
ASIA (VOLUME 7) • BARLEY (VOLUME 10)
MAYAN CIVILIZATION (VOLUME 4)

SEARCH LIGHT

Find and correct the error in the following sentence: Maize was first found in Europe.

DID YOU KNOW?
None of the maize plant has to be wasted. For example, the stalks are made into paper and materials for building. And the cobs - the spikes stripped of kernels - are used for fuel and to make charcoal.

Vast fields of maize like this one in the U.S. state of Nebraska are a common sight in the U.S. Corn Belt.
© Philip Gould/Corbis

Answer: Maize was first found in the Americas.

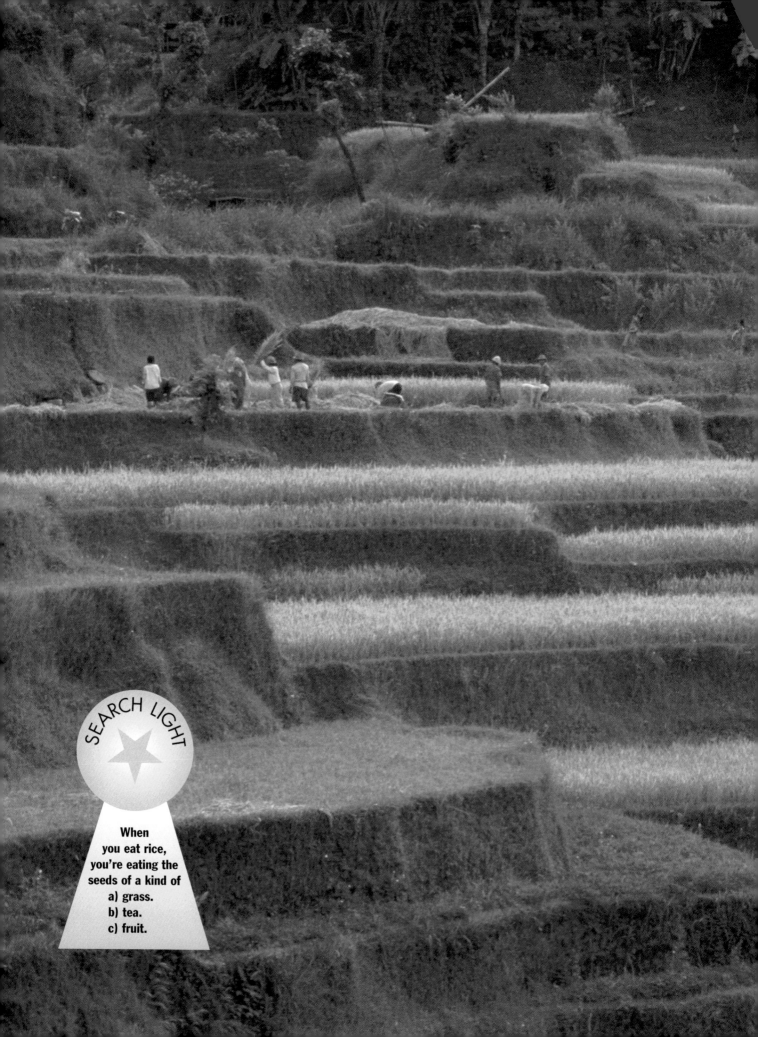

Food from Water-Grown Grasses

Do you chew grass? Actually, you probably do! The grains that most people eat daily are actually grasses - or at least grass seeds. These include wheat, maize, rye, and rice. More than half the people in the world eat rice almost every day. The grain is so important that millions of people in Asia would starve if they didn't have it. China and India are amongst the largest producers of rice. Rice is also the basic feature of most meals in the islands of the western Pacific and much of Latin America.

Rice plants are carried for planting.
© Michael S. Yamashita/Corbis

Most rice is grown in water. The land under the water has to be smooth and level, like a table top. The water on top must be the correct depth. If it's too deep, the rice will drown. If it's not deep enough, the rice won't grow.

In the countries of Asia, the muddy ground is ploughed by water buffalo pulling wooden ploughs. Then the tiny rice plants are planted in rows. If it doesn't rain enough, water is brought in from lakes and rivers to flood the fields. The rice plant grows under the water, with its green shoots sticking out. A water-filled field planted with rice is called a 'rice paddy'.

When the rice is ripe, the water is drained off the fields. After the ground has dried, the rice **stalks** are cut and tied into bundles. When the stalks have dried, the brown **hulls** are removed from the rice seeds. Many farmers grow rice for their families to eat. Rice to be sold in shops goes to a factory. There it is packed into boxes and then shipped to the shops.

DID YOU KNOW?
Rice was first grown as a crop about 5,000 years ago in India. It later spread from there. It reached southern Europe in the 1400s.

LEARN MORE! READ THESE ARTICLES...
BUFFALO (VOLUME 12) • CHINA (VOLUME 7) • GRASSES (VOLUME 10)

In order to grow rice in hilly areas, giant steps called 'terraces' are dug into the hillsides. Each giant step has a little wall of mud at its edge to hold in the water that covers the rice as it is growing.
© Dave G. Houser/Corbis

Answer: a) grass.

Large wheat fields cover parts of Kansas, North Dakota, Montana, Oklahoma, and Washington in the United States.
© Joseph Sohm; ChromoSohm Inc./Corbis

SEARCH LIGHT

About how many years ago was wheat first grown on farms?
a) 9,000
b) 900
c) 9,000,000

The Bread of Life

Wheat is one of the oldest and most important of the **cereal** crops. Many people eat wheat products at every meal. It is an important ingredient of many breads, pastries, and pastas. Wheat has lots of **nutrients** and is a major source of energy for humans.

Wheat ready for harvesting.
© Bohemian Nomad Picturemakers/Corbis

Wheat can be eaten simply by soaking and cooking the seeds, or grain. But for many foods the grain has to be turned to flour first. This requires grinding the wheat.

The wheat plant is a kind of grass with long slender leaves. In most kinds of wheat the stems are hollow. The top part of the plant is made up of a number of flowers. Two to six flowers form groups called 'spikelets'. Two to three of the flowers in each spikelet produce grains. It's the grains that are used as food.

More of the world's farmland is used for growing wheat than for any other food crop. The world's largest producer of wheat is China. Other leading producers are India, the United States, Russia, France, Ukraine, and Turkey.

Many thousands of varieties of wheat are known. The most important ones are used to make bread and pasta. Club wheat, a soft variety, is used for cakes, biscuits, pastries, and household flour.

Wheat was first grown on farms about 9,000 years ago in the Euphrates River valley of the Middle East. In ancient Egypt, wheat was so important that the people buried some with the pharaohs (kings). In this way, they believed, the pharaohs would never go hungry in the afterlife.

DID YOU KNOW?
Although most wheat is eaten, some of it is used to make paste. (Be careful not to confuse the two!)

LEARN MORE! READ THESE ARTICLES…
EGYPT: THE PHARAOHS AND THE PYRAMIDS (VOLUME 8)
FERTILE CRESCENT (VOLUME 7) • GRASSES (VOLUME 10)

A Sweet and Syrupy Plant

The sugarcane plant is a giant grass that grows year-round in warm and wet regions of the world. The island of New Guinea is probably the original home of sugarcane. Gradually, the plant was introduced to Southeast Asia, India, Polynesia, and other areas. Today Asia is the largest producer of sugarcane, followed by South and North America.

Workers harvesting sugarcane.
© Otto Lang/Corbis

The sugarcane plant is grown for its sweet **sap**. Much of the world's sugar and molasses comes from sugarcane sap. And in many parts of the world, people enjoy sucking on a piece of sugarcane for a sweet treat.

Sugarcane grows in clumps of stalks that reach a height of 3 to 6 metres. The colour of the stalk varies from almost white to yellow to deep green, purple, red, or violet.

The sugarcane crop needs at least 150 centimetres of water per year and nine months for the stalks to ripen. Once the stalks are ripe, they are stripped of their leaves and trimmed. The stalks are then washed and cut into short lengths. Most of this work is still done by hand.

Sugar is removed from the cane by two methods. In the first method, the finely cut stalks are put in hot water. This separates the sugar from the stalks. In the second method, the juice is squeezed from the stalks by pressing them between heavy rollers.

The juice taken from the cane is heated until it is boiling. Next, the water in the juice is allowed to **evaporate**. The resulting syrup is boiled again until sugar crystals have formed. The syrup left behind is called 'molasses'.

DID YOU KNOW?

Raw sugar is brown, not white.

LEARN MORE! READ THESE ARTICLES...
ASIA (VOLUME 7) • CACAO (VOLUME 10) • MAPLE (VOLUME 10)

Sugarcane is sold at market in a village in India.
© Earl & Nazima Kowall/Corbis

SEARCH LIGHT

Fill in
the gaps:
We get
_____ and
_____ from
sugarcane sap.

Answer: We get sugar and molasses from sugarcane sap.

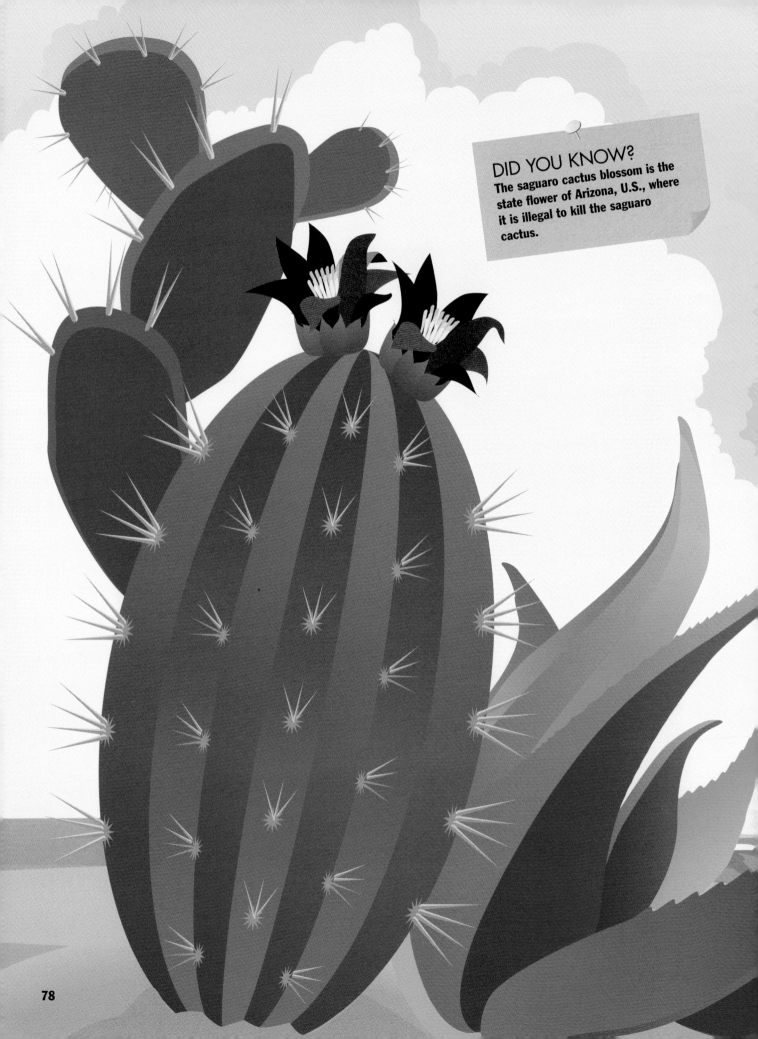

DID YOU KNOW?
The saguaro cactus blossom is the state flower of Arizona, U.S., where it is illegal to kill the saguaro cactus.

Don't Touch!

Cactus plants nearly always grow in dry areas where it hardly ever rains. In all there are about 1,650 different kinds of cactus plants (cacti). All of them except one live in North and South America, especially in Mexico. Cacti can be very tall or really tiny. Some have strange shapes or features. In the Arizona desert of the United States, you can see miles of giant treelike saguaro cacti. Another type, the old-man cactus, got its name from its woolly white 'hair'. Some prickly pear cacti have a fruit that can be eaten. You can even make sugary sweets from a cactus.

Most plants give off water through their leaves. But water is rare and **precious** in the deserts where cacti live. Cacti save water by having no leaves or only small ones that drop off early. A cactus also stores up water inside its thick stem. Almost every cactus has sharp spines that look like thorns or needles. These help protect it from people and animals that want to eat the moist parts inside. In the old days in the American West, the watery juice inside a barrel cactus often saved people's lives.

Some types of cacti are used for making medicines. Dried-up cacti are sometimes used as firewood, and cacti planted around houses can provide a thorny fence. Many people like to keep cacti as houseplants for their unusual appearance. Some cacti also produce big colourful flowers. Maybe you could grow a cactus garden!

LEARN MORE! READ THESE ARTICLES…
DESERTS (VOLUME 1) • MEXICO (VOLUME 9) • PORCUPINES (VOLUME 12)

SEARCH LIGHT

There are more than how many different kinds of cacti in the world?
a) 650
b) 16,500
c) 1,650

DID YOU KNOW?
The cedar tree is featured on the flag of Lebanon. In early historic times cedars of Lebanon were plentiful throughout the area.

A Sweet-Smelling Wood

The cedar is an evergreen tree that grows in the mountains. There are four kinds of cedar. Three of them - including the cedar of Lebanon - originally grew only in the mountain areas of the Mediterranean. They later spread to other areas. The fourth kind grows in the Himalayas, a mountain system in South Asia.

Fill in the gap: Cedar wood is used to make clothing chests because its scent is supposed to keep _____ out.

Cedars are tall trees with large trunks and huge heads of spreading branches. They usually grow to a height of about 15 metres. The leaves are stiff and needle-like. They are scattered along the branches in clusters. Each cluster may have as many as 30 needles. The cedar tree also bears large barrel-shaped cones. The cones are greenish or purplish and are covered with woody scales. The cones hold the seeds that can grow new cedars.

Forest worker sampling a cedar tree.
© Walter Hodges/Corbis

Cedar wood has been used for building for a very long time. In fact, people were building with cedar wood even before the great pyramids of ancient Egypt were built. The wood is light and soft and lasts for a long time. It is very sturdy and stands up to all kinds of weather. It has a pretty reddish colour, is easy to work with, and has a pleasant smell.

Many other trees that have sweet-scented wood are commonly called cedars. But they may actually belong to the cypress or juniper family. The scented wood of these cedars has long been popular for making clothing chests and closets because the smell is supposed to keep insects out. Cedar oil is even used in perfumes because of its strong scent.

LEARN MORE! READ THESE ARTICLES…
BEIRUT, LEBANON (VOLUME 7) • KENYA (VOLUME 8) • PINE (VOLUME 10)

Western red cedar trees grow in the Hoh Rain Forest in Olympic National Park in Washington state, U.S.
© Michael T. Sedam/Corbis

Answer: Cedar wood is used to make clothing chests because its scent is supposed to keep insects out.

81

Cotton has long been an important crop in the American South. These cotton plants are being harvested in the state of Mississippi.

SEARCH LIGHT

Find and correct the error in the following sentence: White puffs of cotton grow on cotton plants inside 'balls'.

Summer Snowballs

Blue jeans are made of cotton. So are T-shirts and socks. The curtains in your room may be cotton, along with the sheets on your bed. And all these items start out as balls of fluff on cotton plants.

Puffs of cotton on the stem of a cotton plant.
© Richard Hamilton Smith/Corbis

In places as different as Egypt, the Czech Republic, India, and the southern United States, you can see fields filled with creamy white and pink cotton flowers. During the summer the petals fall off the flowers, and green knobs, or 'bolls', appear. Inside the bolls, white cotton is growing. These bolls grow big and turn dry and brown. Then they burst open, and thick white puffs of cotton with little seeds in them spring out. Suddenly the fields look like fields of snowballs.

Then it's time to pick the cotton. This is done either by hand or by a machine like a **tractor** with a big basket at the back. Handpicking results in a higher-quality **harvest**. But machines are less expensive to use. As a machine moves through the field, it pulls the cotton from the bolls. The cotton gets sucked up through large tubes and dropped into the big basket.

After the cotton is picked, it is sent to a 'cotton gin'. The gin takes the seeds out of the cotton. The cotton is then cleaned, packed tightly in heavy bundles called 'bales', and shipped to factories to be made into thread. The cotton cloth woven from the thread makes good clothing because it is cool and comfortable and easy to wash.

Cotton seeds are important too. They are sold to make margarine, salad oil, food for farm animals, and many other things. And, of course, they're used to plant more cotton.

DID YOU KNOW?
In 1793 Mrs. Samuel Slater became the first woman to file for a U.S. patent. The patent was for a new kind of cotton thread.

LEARN MORE! READ THESE ARTICLES…
NILE RIVER: EGYPT'S GIFT (VOLUME 8)
SHEEP (VOLUME 12) • WEAVING (VOLUME 2)

Answer: White puffs of cotton grow on cotton plants inside 'bolls'.

Most species of eucalyptus have long, slender leathery leaves. Eucalyptus trees are plentiful in areas of Kakadu National Park in Australia's Northern Territory.

SEARCH LIGHT

Find and correct the error in the following sentence: The eucalyptus tree is the tallest tree in the world.

Australia's Gum Trees

The giant gum trees of Australia are among the tallest trees in the world. Only two trees grow taller: the Douglas fir (of North America and Asia) and the giant redwoods (of North America). The giant gum can grow to be 90 metres tall. In Australia 'gum tree' and 'stringybark tree' are names for the eucalyptus tree.

The name 'eucalyptus' comes from two Greek words that mean 'well-covered'. The name probably refers to the tight-fitting cap that covers the eucalyptus flower until it is ready to bloom. There are nearly 500 kinds of eucalyptus. Common varieties include the ironbark, blue gum, jarrah, and Sydney peppermint. Eucalyptus flowers vary from creamy white to yellow to many shades of pink and red.

The trees originally grew only in Australia, New Zealand, and Tasmania and on nearby islands. You can find them now in other warm areas of the world. They are popular in the warmer parts of the Americas and Europe and in northern Africa.

Eucalyptus trees grow rapidly. That is one reason why they are planted along streets and are used as **windbreaks**. The trees also are planted in certain areas to keep the soil from washing away. Eucalyptus wood is used as lumber for outdoor building projects because the wood resists water damage.

Some kinds of eucalyptus are especially useful because of the oil found in their leaves. Eucalyptus oil is used in many medicines, especially in cough syrups and **inhalers**. And one of the most popular animals in Australia loves the eucalyptus tree. Eucalyptus leaves are almost the only thing that koalas eat.

DID YOU KNOW?

Not only do koalas eat eucalyptus leaves, but they also live in the eucalyptus trees.

Eucalyptus leaves.
© Australian Picture Library/Corbis

LEARN MORE! READ THESE ARTICLES…
ADDIS ABABA, ETHIOPIA (VOLUME 8)
CANBERRA, AUSTRALIA (VOLUME 7) • KOALAS (VOLUME 12)

Answer: The eucalyptus tree is the third tallest tree in the world.

85

SEARCH LIGHT

How does moss help prevent floods?

The Thirsty Plant

It's soft and green and spreads over the ground like grass, but it isn't grass. This soft green stuff grows on wood too, but it isn't leaves. It even grows on rocks. It likes the shade, and it's thirsty. It's always thirsty. It's moss.

Moss forming on a decaying log.
© David Muench/Corbis

There are many different types of moss. Some of these plants are very tiny, while others grow more than one metre long. Many mosses rise just barely above the ground. Most mosses are green, but some are red or reddish-brown.

Moss can be found all over the world, from swamps to high mountains, forests, and even deserts. But most moss grows in moist places. It soaks up water and holds it, somewhat like a sponge. And it's good that it does. Whole villages might be flooded if the mountain mosses didn't drink up some of the melted snow in the springtime. Early American pioneers once stuffed moss between the cracks of their log cabins. The tiny moss stems and leaves drank up the raindrops. This helped keep the cabins warm and dry.

Usually, you'll see many of these plants growing very closely together. This helps them store more water. Mosses can be found growing in dark caves or on rotting logs or wet cliff walls. Some kinds cover the forest floor like a carpet. Another type of moss, called 'peat moss', is found in swamps or bogs. When dead peat moss plants decay, or break down, they form a substance called 'peat'. Peat is dried and burned for fuel.

DID YOU KNOW?
Birds line their nests with moss, which they can pick easily. Unlike most plants, moss doesn't have roots that go deep into the ground.

LEARN MORE! READ THESE ARTICLES…
FLOODS (VOLUME 1) • SPONGES (VOLUME 11) • SWAMPS (VOLUME 1)

Mosses are often found on wet boulders and on dripping cliffs in steep, narrow valleys and passages.
© Pat O'Hara/Corbis

Answer: Moss helps prevent floods by soaking up water, such as from melting snow.

Pine trees grow in a rainforest in Alaska.

SEARCH LIGHT

True or false? The leaves of a pine tree stay green even in the winter.

A Useful, Long-Lived Tree

Some pine trees are among the oldest living trees on Earth. In fact, the oldest living tree we know of is a bristlecone pine that's about 4,800 years old.

Pines are found in mountainous places and the cool areas of the Northern **Hemisphere** (the northern half of the Earth). There are around 90 varieties of pine. You may recognize pines from their cones, the hard scaly clusters that are sometimes used for decorations in the winter. Pine trees look like spruce and fir trees, which belong to the same family and also grow cones.

Umbrella pine trees in Donana National Park near Seville, Spain.
© Andrew Brown—Ecoscene/Corbis

There are two kinds of pine tree: soft pines and hard pines. Both kinds have needle-like leaves that stay green all year-round. Soft pines have needles that grow in bunches of five. Their cones have no prickles on them. The wood of these trees is soft and easy to cut. Hard pines have needles growing in groups of two or three. Their cones are covered in prickles. These trees have hard wood that is difficult to cut but lasts for a long time.

There are several ways pine trees can be damaged. The trees catch fire very easily, and they can get sick if they catch diseases caused by **fungi**. Also, insects - such as sawflies, bark beetles, and caterpillars - can chew through parts of the trees.

People use pines for many things. Their wood is used in construction as well as for making paper products. Resin, a liquid from the wood, makes **turpentine**, paints, and varnishes. Some pine seeds are sold as nuts for eating.

DID YOU KNOW?
Some kinds of pine tree can actually benefit from fire because the heat opens their cones and releases their seeds.

LEARN MORE! READ THESE ARTICLES...
CEDAR (VOLUME 10) • INSECTS (VOLUME 11) • PAPER (VOLUME 2)

Answer: TRUE. The tree's leaves are its needles, and they remain green year-round.

A Tree with Bounce

More than 200 years ago, an English chemist named Joseph Priestley received a gift from an American friend: a ball that bounced. Besides being bouncy, the ball could rub away pencil marks. Priestley had never seen anything like it before. He named the new material 'rubber'.

Latex drips out of a rubber tree.
© Neil Rabinowitz/Corbis

The ball was made from the milky sap of a tree that came to be known as the rubber tree. The tree was first found growing in Brazil. Now it's grown in many places, such as Malaysia, Indonesia, and Thailand and parts of India and China.

Rubber trees need heavy rainfall of at least 250 centimetres per year. And they can grow only in areas where frost doesn't form. Only tropical areas can give the rubber tree all that it needs to survive.

Wild rubber trees may reach a height of 37 metres. But rubber trees that people raise on **plantations** grow only to about 24 metres. The people who grow these trees make sure that leaves grow only at the top. This makes the **tapping** of the tree easier.

To tap a rubber tree, workers shave off a slanted strip of bark halfway around the tree. The milky **sap**, called 'latex', then flows out along the cut until it reaches a spout. Finally it drops into a collection cup. Rubber trees can be tapped for latex for up to 30 years. But the trees get to rest between tappings.

LEARN MORE! READ THESE ARTICLES...
BRAZIL (VOLUME 9) • MAPLE (VOLUME 10) • PALM (VOLUME 10)

SEARCH LIGHT

Why do you think Joseph Priestley named the mystery material 'rubber'?

An Indonesian woman cleans a groove in the bark of a rubber tree to help increase the flow of the milky liquid called 'latex'.
© Dean Conger/Corbis

DID YOU KNOW?

Before being used, most rubber is treated with heat and the substance called 'sulfur'. This process is called 'vulcanization'. It was named after Vulcan, the Roman god of fire.

Answer: Priestley called the new material rubber because it could rub away pencil marks.

SEARCH LIGHT

There are many different kinds of seaweed. Can you name three of them?

Wild Plants of the Ocean

You are in the waves at the seaside when suddenly something that feels cold and clammy slaps you on the back! Is it a friendly fish? No, it's probably just seaweed. These plants grow wild in the sea, just as weeds grow wild on land.

Seaweed on a New Zealand beach.
© Richard Hamilton Smith/Corbis

Seaweed grows all over the world. Some kinds float along the top of the water. Others are attached to the sea bottom or to rocks. Seaweed comes in many colours, such as red, brown, purple, and green. It may look like a red carpet or like tree branches with leaves and berries. The 'berries' are actually little gas-filled balloons that help keep the leaves afloat. Some kinds of seaweed, called 'kelp', can grow longer than 30 metres and have tough and leathery branches. Other kinds look like lettuce and are actually called 'sea lettuce'.

People have found many uses for seaweed. The plants have been used for stuffing furniture and making paper. Giant kelps have been used as ropes. Laver, dulse, gulfweed, sea lettuce, and other kinds of seaweed are eaten, either by themselves or as part of other foods. Brown seaweed is used for making **fertilizers** for plants.

Even animals take advantage of seaweed. Tangled clumps of seaweed provide homes and hiding places for fish and other sea creatures. In the Atlantic Ocean, a huge floating mass of gulfweed between the United States and Africa is a resting place for seabirds. This gulfweed is called *Sargassum*, and this part of the Atlantic is the famous Sargasso Sea.

DID YOU KNOW?
If you like sushi or maki rolls, then you've probably eaten seaweed. Many of these Japanese delicacies are wrapped in seaweed.

LEARN MORE! READ THESE ARTICLES...
GULLS (VOLUME 11) • OCEANS (VOLUME 1) • RUSHES AND REEDS (VOLUME 10)

Giant kelp grows off the coast of California.
© Ralph A. Clevenger/Corbis

Answer: Kelp, sea lettuce, laver, dulse, and gulfweed are all names for different kinds of seaweed.

ambassador person who officially represents his or her own government in a foreign country

brew to prepare by steeping (soaking) or boiling in hot water

calorie unit that measures the amount of heat energy that food provides to the body

carbohydrates plentiful, energy-producing natural substances that are formed by many food plants eaten by animals

cereal starchy seeds of certain grass plants grown for food

citrus kind of tree or shrub grown in warm regions and having thick rind (skin) and fleshy fruits, including oranges, grapefruits, and lemons

climate average weather in a particular area

concentrated condensed, or made thicker, by removing water

cultivate to plant crops and to care for them as they grow

cutting section of an adult plant capable of developing into a new individual

disc the central part of certain flower heads, as in daisies and sunflowers; the discs, in turn, are surrounded by ray flowers

dome large rounded structure shaped like half of a ball

evaporate to change into a vapour or gaseous form, usually by means of heating

evergreen (adjective) having leaves that remain green and working through winter and more than one growing season

exotic unusual and unfamiliar

fertilizer natural or artificial substance used to make soil better for growing crops

fibre strand or thread-like structure

flourish to grow successfully; to do well

fodder coarse food for farm animals

foliage the leaves of a plant

fragrance (adjective: fragrant) sweet, pleasant, and often flowery or fruity smell

fungus (plural: fungi) organism (such as a mushroom or mould) similar to a plant but lacking a stem, roots, leaves, and the substance called 'chlorophyll'

harvest the gathering of a crop

hemisphere half of the planet Earth or any other globe-shaped object

herb pleasant-smelling plant (such as mint, oregano, basil, and coriander) often used in cooking, either in part or as a whole

hull hard outer shell of a seed; also, the outer layer of a boat or ship

husk usually thin dry outer covering of a fruit or seed

inhaler device through which medicine is drawn in through the nose or mouth

kernel whole grain or seed of a cereal plant

marmalade clear, usually sugary jelly containing pieces of fruit and fruit rind

medicinal used as a medicine

native living or growing naturally in a particular region

nursery place where plants are grown for farming, for scientific experiments, or for sale to the public

nutrient substance that a living thing needs in order to stay healthy and grow

plantation large farming property, usually worked by resident labourers

pleated folded and laid over another part of some material, especially a piece of cloth

poultry birds reared for their eggs or meat

precious of great value or high price

prehistoric having to do with times before written history

pulp the juicy fleshy part of a soft fruit; also, a mashed-up pasty glop such as the plant material used in making paper

repel to force away or resist

rind the usually hard or tough outer layer or 'skin' of a fruit or vegetable

sap the liquid inside a plant

saw-toothed having an edge or outline like the teeth (cutting points) of a saw

spout tube, pipe, or hole through which liquid flows

stalk plant's main stem

starchy containing starch, a natural substance that is made by green plants and is part of many foods

Stone Age the oldest period in which human beings are known to have existed, characterized by the making of stone tools

tallow the solid fat of cattle and sheep, used chiefly in making soap, margarine, and candles

tap (verb) to make a hole in something in order to remove the liquid inside

thatch to cover the roof of a building with plant material such as straw

tractor heavy vehicle used to pull farm equipment

train (verb) in gardening and farming, to direct the growth of a plant, usually by bending, trimming, and tying off

tropical having to do with the Earth's warmest and most humid (moist) climates

tuft in plants, a small cluster of flexible leaves or fibres that are attached or close together at the base and free at the opposite end

turban head covering made of a long cloth wrapped around the head or around a close-fitting cap

turpentine oil used to dissolve or thin out paint and other substances

universal present or occurring everywhere

wildlife manager scientist who watches over the conditions, habitats, and populations of wild animals and plants